The Depth of Love

Cover design by Trevor Mason
Cover photograph © Mark Gyde

British Library Cataloguing in Publication Data
ISBN: 978-0-9567792-5-0

The Depth of Love

"Mark, you've learned to be a servant but God wants you to be a son"

One short sentence, but one which changed so much.

Many of us have learned to be servants and actually become quite good at it. Yet we all need to hear those words. We all need to hear the Father calling us by name and speaking these words into our hearts: "you are my beloved son", "you are my beloved daughter". When those words take root in our hearts then everything changes. We begin to discover the amazing depth of the Father's love and can start to live in the reality of Jesus' final words before he was taken to the cross.

This is the depth of love

Mark Gyde

"I have revealed to them who you are and I will continue to make you even more real to them, so that they may experience the same endless love that you have for me, for your love will now live in them, even as I live in them"
(John 17:26 TPT)

To Fiona
My wife, best friend and companion
for these last thirty one years

Dedicated to my family:
Frances and Rich, Hilary, Hannah and John
May you, too, know the depth of Father's
unending love

I love you all.....

CONTENTS

Foreword

I have known Mark for many years. He has been a good friend, a trusted confidant and a real life example to me of what it means to walk in the Spirit of Sonship. His life experience of walking as a beloved son has taken him on a journey which I have been privileged to be a part of.

Mark's new book, "The Depth of Love" wonderfully expresses this growing revelation of sonship and is a natural progression to his first two books (A Father to You and Planted in Love). Mark doesn't shy away from some of the tough topics like hardship and suffering but deals with them in a very practical way. With the help of the Holy Spirit, Mark has been able to put substance to the eternal love which predates creation, in order that we can tangibly experience it in our everyday lives.

Mark is a gifted communicator who shares from the riches of his own life. It is not head knowledge that he writes about, but heart revelation. This book will encourage you, equip you and fan into the flame your hunger to experience more of God's love than you have ever encountered before.

I highly recommend this book to anyone who is longing to go deeper into the immeasurable ocean of Trinitarian love that Jesus Christ secured for us on a cross two thousand years ago.

I am so glad that Mark wrote this book so that we can all experience a deeper awakening to the depths of love that the Father has so freely poured out on all his kids. May you be richly blessed as you read this book with the eyes of your heart open wide.

In Father's love
Barry Adams – Fatherheart.TV and author of the Father's Love Letter

Chapter 1

The Depth of Love

"How deep the Father's love for us
How vast beyond all measure"
© Stuart Townend, 1995 Thank You Music

It started in January 1982 at a young people's holiday in the Lake District.

That was when someone said a single sentence to me which I now see was the start of my journey into Father's love. At the time I knew the sentence was significant and from that point on it began to change my understanding of who God really was. Not only did it change my understanding but it also changed my personal relationship with God. This sentence was not said with any ceremony; it was simply a prophetic statement that came straight from the heart of God.

For the next twenty years that single sentence stayed with me and the impact of it became a foundation of my life. It put within me a yearning to know the reality of who God was and to experience him in a deeper way. It put within me a search for a language that I knew must exist but it was one that I was not hearing.

It took until May 2002 before I heard this language being spoken for the first time and suddenly so many things started to make sense. It seemed as if a whole load of verses started to appear in my Bible which I was sure had not been there before. In that one week relationship replaced religion and a door opened that has become, for me at least, the path of life.

In January 1982 that simple sentence was:

"Mark, you've learned to be a servant but God wants you be a son".

What happened on that evening was one of the leaders from our group of churches came up to me after a meeting, he knelt down on the floor in front of me, put his hands on my shoulders, looked into my eyes and said those few words. Then he got up and walked away! Just a few seconds but in them an impartation of life and a snapshot of not only my destiny and identity but the true destiny and identity of every believer.

We all need to hear those words.

In the coming chapters I am going to explore how those words can become a reality for you in the same way that they have for me. When the power of those words settle in our hearts everything changes and will go on changing. We begin to live in and experience the endless love of the Father. In fact, Jesus' last words before he was taken away to the cross were:

"I have revealed to them who you are and I will continue to make you even more real to them, so that they may experience the same endless love that you have for me, for your love will now live in them, even as I live in them" (John 17:26 TPT)

We are loved in exactly the same way as Jesus is loved. We are loved with the same passion and intensity of love that the Father has for Jesus. This is the depth of the Father's love and this is what we live for.

However, this is not the reality for most Christians. We have settled for, and been taught, a servant hearted or orphan hearted Christianity. I do not believe this has been done consciously or deliberately but it is the result of the subtle deception which took place in the garden way back in Genesis 3.

I wonder what any one of us would have done if we'd been in the garden instead of Adam and his wife. Suddenly they were faced with an angelic being, albeit a fallen angelic being, and I'm sure they were stunned by his beauty. This beauty is described for us in Ezekiel 28 and it must have been breath-taking in its splendour. Lucifer, or Satan as we now know him, was very wise but that wisdom had become corrupted and distorted. In that moment, when he offered the fruit to the woman, Satan offered mankind the fallen, corrupted wisdom that now defined his nature and character.

The woman took it and then she offered it to Adam who was standing right at her side, doing nothing to protect her. It was only once he had taken it that their eyes collectively were opened and the knowledge of good and evil entered the heart of humanity.

Prior to this encounter in the garden Adam and his wife were living in an environment of perfect love. They knew God as their Father and I believe they lived in the fullness of the relationship which Jesus describes in John

14:20 when he says: *"on that day you will realise that I am in my Father and you are in me and I am in you"*. They enjoyed an intimacy of relationship which the Trinity had lived in for all eternity. This is the life of a son or daughter – to enjoy unity and life with the Father, Son and Holy Spirit.

Yet in the garden a choice was made. They gave up everything they had enjoyed in order to obtain the ability to judge right from wrong and good from evil. To sacrifice that unity, love and relationship Satan must have made the alternative very attractive.

The lie we believed was one that said "God can't be trusted, you need to work life out for yourself". Sadly that lie has continued to be sold throughout history and in some way has affected us all.

In the garden an exchange took place: we had previously lived from the heart and now we began to live from the mind. The eyes of our heart began to close and the eyes of our mind began to open. All of which is why Paul prays, in Ephesians 1:18, that the eyes of our heart may be opened so we can once again see and believe who we really are. He also writes in

Ephesians 4:23 that our minds need to undergo a renewal in order that we can be clothed in Christ, which is to be clothed in love.

The lie was that we could work it all out for ourselves and so we stepped outside of the relationship of perfect love and followed the master deceiver and the ultimate orphan, Satan. This lie has subtly affected every area of life: politics, education, social justice, economics, media and culture and, yes, the life of the church itself.

We have exchanged a lifetime of living in love for a man-made system. We build our own kingdoms with our own rules and we place ourselves at the centre; using our 'gift' of corrupted wisdom we try to judge what is right and what is wrong. It is an impossible job for us to do and Satan knew that was the case when he sold us the lie.

And here I am going to make an very important point. Yes, the lie was sold to the whole human race; yes, we have created orphan hearted systems and orphan hearted churches. **But this is not purely an institutional problem, it is a personal one.**

This is about my heart, your heart, our hearts.

We must not look at everything or everyone else as being the problem. Let's look at ourselves.

It is possible for us to regain what has been lost and we need to regain it individually as that is the only way it will grow into a corporate expression of life. As you and I regain and live in the spirit of sonship, as we understand what the ongoing experience of being loved is really like, then collectively we will become the body and family of Christ. The corporate expression of life can only come from the lives of renewed sons and daughters who have discovered the depth of Father's love for them personally.

What we gave away through Adam we can recover through Jesus. To paraphrase John 14, Jesus tells his disciples that he is returning to his Father, he will then send the Holy Spirit of Sonship who will live in us to confirm to us that we are no longer orphans but sons and daughters.

We gave away the opportunity of living in love and this is restored to us as we rediscover the perfect love of the Father. Not a theoretical rediscovery but the impartation of his love into our hearts so we live in the continual experience of him loving us. Paul puts it so well in Ephesians 3:14-19 (TPT):

"So when I think of the wisdom of his plan I kneel humbly in awe before the Father of our Lord Jesus, the Messiah, the perfect Father of every father and child in heaven and on the earth. And I pray that he would pour out over you the unlimited riches of his glory and favor until supernatural strength floods your innermost being with his divine might and explosive power.

Then, by constantly using your faith, the life of Christ will be released deep inside you, and the resting place of his love will become the very source and root of your life, providing you with a secure foundation that grows and grows.

Then, as your spiritual strength increases, you will be empowered to discover what every holy one experiences—the great magnitude of the astonishing love of Christ in all its dimensions. How deeply intimate and far-reaching is his love! How enduring and inclusive it is! Endless love beyond measurement, beyond academic knowledge—this extravagant love pours into you until you are filled to overflowing with the fullness of God!"

"The resting place of his love becomes the very source and root of your life, providing you with a secure foundation that grows and grows". Planting our lives in love is the start of this journey where we can begin to see and experience the depth of his endless love for us.

What I heard in May 2002 was the language of love. It took the sentence which had been spoken over me twenty years earlier and gave it a substance and a reality. Over the next six months I drank this in until I came to a place where I thought I knew everything there was to know about Father's love. How wrong I was! I now know that I have barely begun to understand the magnitude of this love.

I have flown from New Zealand to the UK via Los Angeles. For the first thirteen hours of the flight all we did was fly over the Pacific Ocean. That's a small picture of the enormity of Father's love. We simply can not fathom it.

During the Welsh Revival the hymn writer, William Rees, wrote these words:

"Here is love, vast as the ocean,
Lovingkindness as the flood,
When the Prince of Life, our Ransom,
Shed for us His precious blood.
Who His love will not remember?
Who can cease to sing His praise?
He can never be forgotten,
Throughout Heav'n's eternal days."

He had seen something of the depth and magnitude of the Father's love. He sees how this love is expressed through Jesus on the cross when the floodgates of Heaven opened to enable *"grace and love, like mighty rivers, poured incessant from above, and Heaven's peace and perfect justice kissed a guilty world in love"*. The rest of the hymn is our response to this amazing love and William Rees ends with these words:

"Thy great love and power on me, drawing out my heart to thee".

His love affects everything and it goes on affecting everything. The experience of Father's love is not a one-off event but it is a lifelong relationship of being loved with perfect and complete love. We will never get our minds around it because it is not meant for our minds; it is meant for our hearts.

In fact, if we ever think we have 'got it' we have minimised it and made it too small.

I invite you to explore and experience the depth of this amazing love, because you too can know you are not a servant but a son or a daughter.

Chapter 2

Jesus Reveals Father's Love

"How can a God of love let all these terrible things happen in the world?"

Behind this question is another lie from the father of lies. He would have us believe that everything bad in the world is caused by God. This reinforces the lie that God is not good nor can he be trusted. It reinforces the lie that, if God can't be trusted, we need to rely on our own strength and our own judgement which, as we have seen, comes from fallen or corrupted wisdom.

At the end of the previous chapter I invited you to explore and experience the depth of the Father's love. To do so we need to go beyond these lies and the wrong impressions of God which have been created for us. We need to discover who God really is and how he wants to relate to us. Thankfully we are given a way to discover who he is and that way is called Jesus.

I love the discussion between Jesus and the disciples at the start of John 14. It's just the sort of chat we probably would have had. Jesus starts off by saying he is about to return to his Father and prepare a place for the disciples and, by extension, for us also. He finishes with these words "And you know the way to where I am going".

Thankfully Thomas steps in. He asks the question all the others were thinking. He asks the question we are probably asking. His question is basically "Jesus, what are you talking about, we don't have a clue where you're going!" That question gives Jesus the opportunity to give us one of the most profound statements we have in scripture.

"I am the Way, the Truth and the Life. No one comes to the Father except through me" (John 14:6)

He does not only show us the way to the Father he became the way. He is not simply a signpost showing us the right path to choose, he is the actual pathway that you and I can walk on. Derek Prince made a powerful observation shortly before his death "a way only has a meaning if it leads to a destination". Jesus is the way, but the Father is the destination.

The destination of our journey has to be the Father.

In our discussion in John 14 Philip takes up the conversation. He helps us as much as Thomas when he blurts out *"show us the Father and that will be enough for us" (John 14:8)*. I always feel slightly sorry for Philip as he is as confused as we would have been. He is trying to grapple with something and to make sense of what Jesus is saying and yet it appears as if Jesus gives him a mild rebuke. It is Philip's desire to have the Father revealed which opens the way for Jesus to carefully explain what is about to happen. Jesus paints a very clear picture of the intimate relationship between Father and Son and then draws us into that relationship. He explains that the Holy Spirit will be sent into our hearts and then we will know that we are no longer orphans.

I think Jesus realises that it is quite hard for the disciples to grasp what he is saying. He is wanting to help us understand this significant truth: that it is all about the Father. In verse 11 he encourages the disciples to believe, but if they can't he points to the miracles he has done and says they are evidence enough of who he is and therefore of who the Father is.

In receiving the Holy Spirit we not only have someone living inside us who guarantees our sonship but we have someone who will teach us everything and remind us of all that Jesus has said (John 14:26).

In this crucial evening before Jesus heads to the cross he is making sure that the disciples understand the purpose of his coming. In helping the disciples he also helps us to see that the single purpose of his coming to earth is to reveal the Father.

Let's explore this some more.

At the end of Matthew 11 Jesus is telling his disciples that, by following him and living like him, they can enjoy a life of rest. This is something we all crave and I believe this life of rest is something that has been stolen from us. If we lose our rest we lose our peace and therefore our freedom as sons and daughters is diminished. This is one of the key ways the enemy seeks to make us ineffective.

Before these famous verses on rest we read something equally significant. We are given some keys to enable us to live as sons and daughters.

"At that time Jesus said, "I praise you, Father, Lord of heaven and earth, because you have hidden these things from the wise and learned, and revealed them to little children. Yes, Father, for this is what you were pleased to do. "All things have been committed to me by my Father. No one knows the Son except the Father, and no one knows the Father except the Son and those to whom the Son chooses to reveal him." (Matthew 11:25-27)

I almost feel that Jesus is smiling as he says these words. The things he has been talking about, the things he has been teaching the people about have been hidden from the 'wise and learned' but have been revealed to those with a childlike heart. It is not our understanding that enables us to enter his kingdom of love, it is our heart attitude. The damage which was done in the garden when we chose to live by the fallen and corrupted wisdom of Satan has not done us any good. Our own judgement or assessment of right and wrong is not the key to entering into this kingdom of love. Our own knowledge is not good enough, it just doesn't work. Jesus sets us free from a performance oriented way of life which is governed by rules and regulations and leads us into a relationship of the heart.

We spend so long trying to become wise and learned and yet Jesus says this is the very thing which hinders us from entering a life of rest. It is good to gain knowledge about things where knowledge is important. As an accountant I need to apply my mind in the best way I can when dealing with my clients' affairs. But it is not knowledge that will lead me into the revelation of the Father; it is a revelation of the heart that is opened up through Jesus being the way.

It is the Father's good pleasure to be hidden from the wise and learned and it is his good pleasure to reveal himself to those with a childlike heart. A childlike heart is one that is dependent on the Father. It is trusting the Father to take care of us through all the circumstances life throws at us. It is the simple belief that we have a good Father who, because of his unending love for us, will provide for us. It is a simplicity of faith which we lose so easily when we try to complicate it with rules and procedures. It is a relationship of love.

To fully understand the depth of Father's love we need to let go of the strength of our mind. We need to lay aside our understanding of what we consider to be right or wrong and come to place our little hand in our Father's hand and then walk with him in love.

One key, therefore is to have a childlike heart. Another key is found in verse 27. *"No-one knows the son except the Father and no-one knows the Father except the son"*. If Jesus had left it there what hope would we have! There would be a cosy Father–Son relationship in which we could not partake. Thankfully, Jesus gives us the next key *"no-one knows the Father except the Son **AND** those to whom the Son chooses to reveal him"*.

We can know the Father because Jesus is in the business of revealing him. There is hope. Jesus is not selective to whom he reveals the Father, he reveals him to anyone who has eyes to see and a heart to know. No-one is excluded as we all have the opportunity to enter into this love relationship with Father. It is Jesus' good pleasure to reveal his Father to orphans who are looking to find their way home.

It is the revelation of the Father which enables us to enter this life of rest. It is the revelation of the Father that enables us to "live freely and lightly, flowing in the unforced rhythms of grace" (as the Message version puts it in Matthew 11:29-30). We will not enter fully into a life of rest if we do not have a revelation of the Father and an understanding of the depth of his love for us.

Let's now take a look at John 17 which is Jesus' prayer shortly before he is taken to the cross. In this prayer Jesus says a number of things which reveal the Father to us.

At the start of the chapter as Jesus prays, he says to his Father that he has finished all the work he was sent to earth to accomplish. This is before the cross and Jesus is saying 'job done'. He has glorified the Father in his life which simply means that Jesus' life has been Father-centred rather than self-centred. Nothing about his life draws attention to him but everything points to the Father. In John 4:34 Jesus states his food is to do the will of his Father. The thing that sustains him or gives him energy is pleasing his Father by doing his will. To me, that begs a question: if it was Jesus' desire to only do his Father's will – what about us? Is it our desire as well?

Jesus has done what he came to do and this is clearly stated in verse 3. He has come to reveal his Father in order that we might know him.

In John 17:6 we read that Jesus has made his Father known which literally means he has made his name known. This sentence is full of meaning as to make someone's name known is far more than a formal introduction over a handshake. It is the revealing of someone's personality, nature and character. It is showing what that other person is really like.

In saying 'job done', Jesus is telling us that part of that job was to reveal the full personality of his Father in order that you and I may know him as Jesus knows him. Not know about him, but know him in our hearts to the same full extent that Jesus knows him. This is a major paradigm shift as, historically, the Israelites only knew about him and now Jesus concludes his ministry by becoming the way for us to enter into relationship with the Father, enabling us to live loved.

In stepping into humanity and living as he did Jesus showed us the Father. He dispelled the myth that God was distant, angry, unapproachable or impersonal. He cancelled the requirement of the law which said only a High Priest could enter God's presence and even then that was on an annual basis. Each time Satan challenged Jesus in the wilderness he refuted the false claims by grounding himself in his identity with his Father. He did not accept or come under the lie which had been sold to the human race in the garden but stood apart from it and showed there was another way.

The Pharisees and teachers of the law wanted to kill Jesus purely because he claimed to be the Son of God. They could see he was revealing a completely different God to the one they had taught about.

The whole of Jesus' life was to reveal his Father. He shows us a loving Father – "*for God so **loved** the world*", he shows us a Father who has compassion for the poor and needy, he shows us a Father who values women and children, he shows us a Father who heals the sick, cares for families in distress, provides for people when they are in need. He shows us a Father who meets people at their point of need and who does not accuse or judge but sets them free. He shows a Father who does not like the divisions in society. He shows a Father who is more concerned with relationship than with any form or organised religion.

When Jesus says 'job done' he is saying "I have revealed who my Father really is and what he is really like".

Another part of Jesus' mission is found in John 17:14 when he says that he has given us the Father's word. Jesus, of course, is the living Word of God and when he read from the prophet Isaiah in Luke 4 he is reading about himself. He came to set the captives free and to proclaim the year of the Lord's favour. As he only did and said what his Father gave him to say we can hear the Father saying that this is the season of freedom and wholeness.

Jesus spoke words of eternal life. Words that set us free rather than condemning us. In John 13 Jesus washes the disciples' feet at the start of their meal together. Peter is not content to have only his feet washed, he wants a full bath. Jesus' reply is that they are already clean and then adds to this in John 15 when he says "*you are already clean because of the word I have spoken to you".*

Jesus is the Word of God, the Word of the Father, and this word brings wholeness to our lives. It gives us purpose and destiny because it is a living word which sets us free and enables us to live as sons and daughters.

When Jesus says 'job done' he is saying that he has given us the Father's word which cleanses and restores us and leads us deeper into sonship.

Reading on, we see in John 17:22-23 that Jesus has set us free to live from the heart because we now live in unity and relationship with the Father. Just as Jesus glorified and honoured his Father, so too he glorifies and honours us as we are brought into this perfect unity. This is something which often eludes us as we do not feel we are worthy enough to be accepted. Jesus is clear: we are one just as the Father and Son are one.

As sons and daughters we are included. No longer are we outside the camp trying hard to win the favour of a master but we are sons and daughters who belong to the family forever. A slave can only point to a master. A son reveals a Father and, as sons and daughters, we too can reveal our Heavenly Father to a hurting and broken world.

The picture of unity and oneness which Jesus paints leads to a declaration that we are loved as Jesus is loved. I'll unpack this amazing revelation in a little while but it clearly points to our true relationship with the Father. This would have been a totally foreign concept to Jesus' listeners who would have barely mentioned the words *God* and *love* in the same sentence. This is a radical statement and one that we should not underestimate.

The final few verses of John 17 build to a crescendo through which we are left in no doubt as to the purpose of Jesus' earthly life and ministry. I believe this is a secret that has been hidden from the wise and learned and can only be seen through the eyes of the heart. Jesus reveals this secret for the first time in many generations. This secret is what being a Christian is all about. This is the reality of our lives as sons and daughters.

Let's begin to unpack this great revelation.

"Father, I want those you have given me to be with me where I am, and to see my glory, the glory you have given me because you loved me before the creation of the world." (John 17:24)

What an amazing statement! The desire of the perfect, righteous, sinless Son of God is that you and I can be with him where he is. In our brokenness and pain, with all our imperfections and failings we can be with the perfect, spotless Son of God. Pause and think about that for a moment. What a gift! Jesus wants us to be with him and sharing in his glory. What an amazing big brother we have!

Jesus knows our brokenness, he knows our weakness, he knows the judgements we make and the criticisms we have yet he still longs for us to be with him. He does not wait for us to be fully healed or restored he simply invites us in.

If we recall the opening chapter of John's gospel we remember that Jesus came from the bosom of the Father (John 1:18). That is the place to which he is returning and that is the place where we are invited to be as we enter into this beautiful love relationship. We are where he is and so (maybe for the first time) we begin to find our true home in his heart.

The grand finale of this revelation of Father is in verse 26. The very last words Jesus spoke before he was taken away to the cross are the climatic summary of his life and ministry. You often hear it said that the last words someone says are very important and this is certainly the case for us as we consider these words of Jesus.

"I have made you known to them, and will continue to make you known in order that the love you have for me may be in them and that I myself may be in them." (John 17:26)

Jesus came to reveal the Father and that is what he has done through his life and his relationships with the people he met. He has made the true nature and personality of the Father known and it has been recorded in great detail in order that you and I can receive this amazing revelation of the Father and live loved.

Not only has Jesus revealed the Father but he continues to reveal the Father which is very good news for us. Every day Jesus reveals the Father, he goes on revealing the Father, he continues to be the way for us to come to Father. This vital ministry has not stopped and we can live in the experience of the Father being revealed to us through Jesus.

When Jesus says 'job done' he is saying that he has shown us who the Father really is, he has torn down the old religious expectations and brought us into a new and living relationship with Father.

Even with all this revelation I am left with a question. The answer to which will take us deeper into the revelation and experience of the Father loving us. It will show us the single purpose of what Jesus came to accomplish. It reveals the depth of the Father's heart for us which has been there since before the beginning of time. It brings about the restoration of his plan for mankind and restores to us everything we lost through Adam.

The question I'm left with is "Why?". Why did Jesus come to reveal the Father?

The answer is found in John 17:26. We are loved. **We are loved by the Father in exactly the same way as Jesus is loved.** It has always been the Father's plan to have a family and when we walked out of the garden in a fallen orphan state he did everything in order to redeem us back to being his sons and daughters. He did it simply because he loves us.

This is the depth of the Father's love revealed to us through Jesus.

"I have given them the revelation of who you are and I will continue to make you even more real to them so that they may experience the same endless love that you have for me; for your love will now live in them, even as I live in them!" (John 17:26 TPT)

Chapter 3

Did The Father Look Away?

"My God, my God, why have you forsaken me?"
The anguished cry of Jesus from the cross!

A cry of despair, of hopelessness. The one who had walked in intimate relationship with his Father now seems to find himself abandoned and alone at his greatest time of need. Can this really be the case?

Let's take a few moments to look at what was really going on.

There is a common train of thought which says the Father could not look on his son once he had taken on himself the sin of the world. I can't even begin to imagine what all the sin of the world looks like: past, present and future. This is impossible for us to imagine. Yet all that sin and darkness was put onto Jesus. In fact, he actually became sin for our sake (2 Corinthians 5:21).

We cannot begin to grasp what all that darkness looks like. The sin of thousands of years and billions or people all rolled up and placed on one man, at a single point in time, on a wooden cross. It would have been the most intense concentration of darkness ever and one that will never be seen or experienced again. There are some 'dark' places in the world today. Places where there is a concentration of evil. Thankfully I have not experienced too much of that personally but I know the feelings I experience when I enter such a place. It is oppressive and I want to get out quickly. I have spoken to people who have experienced much more intense darkness than I have but these simply do not compare with the intensity of sin that Jesus bore as he became the Way for us to come back home to the Father.

What Jesus did is beyond our understanding, but he did it because of his love for his Father and his eternal desire to see us brought back home.

With all that sin on one person it is quite understandable to think the Father turned his face away. But did he?

I think we interpret this through our human perspective. None of us could look on that much sin and darkness, it would be humanly impossible, and so we think that neither could God.

My fundamental question is "if God can't look on sin what hope is there for us?"

God is not afraid of sin, it does not cause him to panic. It does not cause him to lose his peace and rest. In fact, he looks on sin every moment of every day because he looks at us!

Having just written that sentence I realise it is written from a human perspective. When God looks at you and me, those of us who have believed in him and appropriated our salvation through the blood of Jesus, he sees us as being **in** Christ with our sin dealt with. In Ephesians 2 Paul describes this new relationship by saying that we are seated in Heavenly places **in** Christ Jesus. As we read through John 14 we see that the Father has chosen to make his home in our hearts. What we see as sinful and broken, God, the Father, sees as his home. This is the Heavenly perspective.

It is important for us to understand that God has always been Father. He does not start being Father the moment we become a Christian. He created each one of us and knew us intimately before we were in our mother's womb. He has always been Father and he longs to bring <u>all</u> his children home. Sadly, many people do not wish to receive the free gift of eternal life and, although their sin continues to separate them from the Father, he continues to woo them in the hope they might find their way home.

Ever since that fateful moment in the garden, God has looked upon the sinful human race, not with judgement, but with love and compassion, longing for us to turn and come home. That desire was fulfilled when his perfect son died on the cross.

Mel Gibson's portrayal of the crucifixion in the Passion was brutal. It presented the most graphic picture of what Jesus could have gone through. A brutal beating few would survive.

When Jesus is hanging on the cross his physical energy is almost spent and his friends have largely abandoned him. Irrespective of the weight of sin his physical body has very little left and for him to say anything is nothing short of a miracle. In this spent and empty state he manages to ask John to look after his mother and his mother to look after John.

With little or no physical capacity he somehow musters enough energy to cry out the opening verse of Psalm 22. *"My God, my God why have you forsaken me?"*

The moment he uttered those words all those watching would have immediately understood the association. Not only would they have connected Jesus' cry to Psalm 22 they would have remembered all words of the psalm. They would have recalled the whole story King David had prophesied all those years before as he looked forward to this moment of Jesus on the cross.

In hearing Jesus' cry from the cross they would have remembered that the Psalmist says in verse 8: *"He trusts in the LORD, let the LORD rescue him. Let him deliver him, since he delights in him."* They would have remembered the words of verses 9 to 11: *"Yet you brought me out of the womb; you made me trust in you, even at my mother's breast. From birth I was cast on you; from my mother's womb you have been my God. Do not be far from me, for trouble is near and there is no one to help"*. In these verses we read of the complete trust and dependence that Jesus had on his Father.

They would remember the prophetic cry as Jesus calls to his Father asking him to be close to his side and helping him in his time of need. *"But you, LORD, do not be far from me. You are my strength; come quickly to help me"* (verse 19).

Most importantly those listening to Jesus on the cross would remember the prophetic declaration that King David cries out in verse 24: *"For he has not despised or scorned the suffering of the afflicted one;* **he has not hidden his face from him but has listened to his cry for help**.*"*

The Father did not turn his face away. He could not turn his face away. He is there with Jesus as he goes through the pain and agony of the cross. I think as Jesus bore the weight of sin he **felt** isolated and alone. But it is in that moment of aloneness that he remembers the prophetic Psalm written by his ancestor and he speaks these words to remind himself and his listeners of the absolute truth; that the Father is always with him just as he is always with us. His broken body, lacking all energy, forces those words out and in doing so he releases a cry of hope and salvation. Instead of abandonment he declares that his Father is with him in every moment of agony which he experiences on that cross.

He already knew that his Father would never forsake or abandon him because, in John 16:32, he tells the disciples that they will be scattered and will all leave him. Yet he will not be alone for *"my Father is with me"*. He is so assured of this fact that when his human body eventually gives up he hands over his spirit, or his heart, to his Father (Luke 23:46).

His final words on the cross are *"it is finished"* and these too are an echo of the final words of Psalm 22 *"he has done it"*.

Psalm 22 is not a story of abandonment but it is a story of hope. It is a story of the Father's presence being with his son and staying with him throughout his time of greatest need. It is a declaration of the Father's absolute love for his son. A love that is not withdrawn when the going is tough but a love that is steadfast and resolute even when Jesus, the son of God, becomes sin.

The Father did not turn his face away and that gives me hope.

If the Father had turned his face away from his beloved son it would imply that the sin of the world was too great for him. This is not the case at all. The Father is bigger than all of the sin of the world. His love knows no bounds. His love endures to all generations and it is this love which he lavishes on us. Generous, unlimited, immeasurable love.

Psalm 22, and the words of Jesus on the cross, remind us that wherever we go or whatever we go through the love of the Father is there for us. He presence is always with us.

He will never leave you or forsake you. There is nothing you can do that will stop him loving you as much as he loves Jesus. Conversely there is nothing you need to do to make him love you any more than he already does.

Through the cross we can see the depth of the Father's love for Jesus. It is that same depth of love which reaches out to you and me, for we are all loved by the Father with the same measure of love as he has for his son, Jesus. It is that depth of love that goes even to the depravity of mankind and invites the darkest and most closed heart to come home. It is that depth of love that draws us home to the heart of the Father, to the place where we find acceptance and belonging.

The Father did not look away from his son and nor will he look away from us. For just as Jesus is the beloved so too are we.

Chapter 4

The Great Confrontation

For most of the time our life and the lives of others appear to be a series of ups and downs. We call this the "stuff of life" but at the time the ups can seem to be very high and the downs very low. We feel them acutely. We are caught up with them and they take over our time, energy and emotions. This can define our routine but then, occasionally, something of such magnitude happens which puts our ups and downs into a bit more perspective. Something takes place on the world stage that is a once in a lifetime event. It truly changes the course of history not just for a few days or weeks but for decades or even centuries to come. I'm not talking about the result of a general election and the change of political leadership, I'm not talking about a new President or King or Queen. I'm talking about something like the fall of the Berlin wall or 'nine-eleven'.

These are events of such magnitude and importance, which happen so rarely, that for a moment we are frozen in time. We all know what we were doing and where we were when they happened. We remember the feelings of shock and maybe horror followed by the realisation that everything has changed, nothing will be the same again. Often such events represent a clash of cultures or ideologies. They are strong forces that clash, impacting us all.

There is such a clash which is played out in John 14. A confrontation occurs that changes everything and affects each one of us if only we can see and hear what is going on. If we allow the eyes of our heart to discern what is happening we will never be the same again. The thing is, this challenge takes place so gently that its power and impact can easily be missed.

A change is taking place.

Imagine for a moment what the disciples must have been feeling as they gathered together in the upper room. For three years they have been with Jesus, they have seen the miracles he has performed and they've watched as he openly confronts the worn out and dead religion of the Pharisees. They have seen his genuine care and love for the people. They've seen people comforted in their anguish, they've seen people healed and provided for. They've watched as he has ushered in a new era that is based on relationship and life rather than dead works, they've heard him refer to Yahweh as his Father. They've seen love in action but now they are aware that something is changing.

The leaders want to kill Jesus and are actively plotting how they can make this happen. In the midst of all this Jesus' conversation starts to change as it takes on a new urgency. He begins to talk about leaving them, of going back to his Father, of a large house with many rooms and then sending another Comforter who will be with them just as he has been with them. This must have been very confusing for the disciples who, after all, were only ordinary men and women.

Jesus would have been aware of their feelings which is why he starts off by saying "do not let your hearts be troubled". Comfort, so important to Jesus, is going to be the central theme of this conversation. Jesus brings peace to his disciples and that is exactly what he wants to do for you and me.

The challenge we are about to see unfold is designed to bring us into a place of peace, rest and security. It is designed to calm our troubled hearts so that the turmoil of our everyday lives can subside. Our understanding of who we are is about to change and as it does we will begin to live from a different place. Henri Nouwen describes it as knowing, in the depth of our hearts, that we are the beloved sons and daughters of the Father. That we can know and experience the same beloved-ness that Jesus lived in. And, Henri Nouwen says, as we experience this beloved-ness we begin to be nurtured in the core of our being and as that nurture grows it eventually envelops the ups and downs of our daily existence. The internal experience of nurture in our lives has an outward expression in the practical reality of our life!

Jesus comforts us and then he postures us so we are looking in the right direction. "Don't be troubled" he says, "believe in me". Where are we looking? It's true, we reflect what we look at which is why we are pointed back to right direction. With turmoil all around it is easy to look at the ups and downs of life and let them shape the state of our heart. Paul encourages us to allow the eyes of our heart to be opened in order that we can begin to know the hope to which we have been called. Here Jesus re-focusses us so that our gaze is on him.

It is at this point that the confrontation begins to unfold. "If you really know me, you will know my Father as well".

Jesus spoke to an age where God was not known as Father. In fact, knowing God as Father was something which had been lost in the garden at the end of Genesis 3. Throughout the whole of the Old Testament there was a cry on God's heart for his people to return to him and discover the truth of who he was. This cry came through Abraham, Moses, the kings and prophets but was largely unheard. Mankind had chosen to follow the ultimate orphan and to walk according to the 'prince of the power of the air' (Ephesians 2:2). The time that Jesus spoke into was not very much different to the one we find ourselves in. In Trevor Galpin's book, 'Finding the Father in the Story of the Church', he gives a very thorough account of the way the Father was lost after the initial revelation to the early church and how there is a new re-discovery beginning to sweep through the church today. Thankfully, the tide is starting to turn and we live in an age where, once again, people are living in the experience of being loved and knowing God being a Father to them.

It is an experience of being loved rather than a doctrine of who God is.

The clarion call from Jesus, which is as real for us as it was for the disciples, is to turn around, see the Father and to find his peace. Jesus challenges our orphan heartedness, he shows us the futility of it and then shows us the best way to live.

The amazing truth Jesus reveals for us is that we can be where he is. We can live where he lives; we can be at home with him. His home is our home too. No longer do we have to live an independent life trying to work it all out on our own but we are drawn into the very life of Christ. We are drawn into Christ so that his home becomes our home. This is an eye to eye and heart to heart relationship. Instead of troubled hearts and turmoil we are drawn into the security of being with him at the Father's side or as one translation says 'in the Father's bosom'. At last we have a home. A true home, a place of identity and intimacy knowing that we truly belong. A place to relax and be ourselves. A place where striving and trouble can cease and one which is ruled by peace and rest. Our true home!

I imagine at this point the disciples felt even more confused and I guess we can feel that way as well. Where is Jesus going? How can we be with him? It's Thomas who comes to help us with his famous question "we don't know where you are going, so how can we know the way?" I am so glad Thomas put his doubts into words as it gives Jesus the opportunity to explain in more detail what is really going on.

Jesus is the Way. As Derek Prince said there is a journey and a destination. The journey has to have a destination, Jesus is the journey or the pathway and the Father is the destination. He went on to say how easy it is for us to become stuck on the journey and to miss the destination. Jesus not only shows us the way, he became the way for us to come to the Father. We are taken into Christ and then he takes us, in himself, to the Father. He is the way and he is also the vehicle for taking you and me to the heart of our perfect Father.

He is the Way and he is also the Truth. Truth is the person of Jesus, it is not a collection of facts or a series of rules for right living. As we come to know him we meet the person of truth who reveals the secrets of our heart in such a loving way which enables us to be set free.

Jesus is the Way, the Truth and also the Life. As we discover the reality of the journey which he takes us on we discover true life. The life we are offered is a full and an abundant one which we will explore together in chapter seven. Previously under our orphan hearted existence we have been under the influence of the thief who only comes to kill, steal and destroy.

The clash which is being played out in John 14 is powerful as it changes everything if we can only understand what is being said. The offer is to know the Father as Jesus knows him. The offer is to turn and gaze upon him. The offer is to turn away from our orphan heartedness and to journey into the Father's heart and make our home with him. Jesus, as our elder brother, leads us into this truth and opens up the way for us to experience an abundant and complete life of freedom.

The story of Cain and Abel powerfully reveals the nature of the orphan heart which has settled on all of humanity. Because of his actions, Cain was sentenced to be a 'restless wanderer' on the face of the earth. What an empty life! No purpose, no identity and no place to call home. For us too this is the state of our heart until we understand and respond to what Jesus is saying throughout John 14. It is only as we respond to this challenge and discover our true home with the Father that this wandering and restlessness in our heart can begin to subside and cease.

This is the confrontation of Jesus' message: continue to live a restless life or turn and discover the way we were really meant to live.

Philip suddenly sees something. He realises that it is all about the Father and in his heart he longs to know the Father Jesus knows and is describing. That same longing can be awakened in our hearts as we too cry out "Jesus, show us the Father and that will be enough". As the eyes of our heart are opened we see the Father just as Philip did and we allow ourselves to be taken to home to the Father. Jesus, always the encourager, gives us hope because even if we struggle to believe he offers his life and miracles as being proof enough that the Father is in him and is with him. We are left in no doubt that Jesus is confronting the orphan hearted ways of humanity and the way we have been living since the garden. Today he is confronting our religious mindset which operates out of the default position of us having to work hard in order to try to please God and win his favour. He is challenging the restless wandering of our heart and he is issuing an invitation for us to come home to the heart of our true Father. He opens the door for us to know that, not only is God a Father, but he is also being a Father to us. Not only is God a God of love but he is loving each one of us now which enables us to live in love and to live loved.

In Philip's statement "show us the Father and that will be enough" there is a question for us all. Is Father enough? Is he all we need?

In some ways it is not possible to answer that question until it is put to the test. I guess many of us would say that in theory he is enough but this can only be proved through our experience. For Jesus the Father was enough. He did not need to seek favour with men, he did not need to perform in order to gain approval, he could challenge the religiousness and hypocrisy of the Pharisees without any fear of man. For him, his Father was enough. As our hearts find their true home with Father we too begin to discover, experience and prove that he really is enough.

Knowing he is enough comes out of a deepening heart relationship, it does not come from a legalistic way of life in which we seek to obey God in order to win his love.

In John 14 Jesus says the same thing three times: "If you love me you will obey me". He has to say it three times because it is so important and he wants us to hear it and grasp it fully. Love comes first. Love creates the atmosphere for obedience to follow, it is not the other way round. Obedience will never create an environment for love, it will only create one of fear. In fact when we live in love obedience ceases to be an issue; rather it becomes us desiring to do Father's will which is totally different to our blind obedience.

Too often we have missed the point. We have majored on obedience and on trying to do the right thing or behave in the right way. We fail and become disheartened because it is impossible to hit the standard we set for ourselves (we disguise it in religious language by thinking it is the standard God sets for us). Obedience is only an issue when there is a point of disagreement or a challenge to conform. With children it is a matter of obedience when they don't do what you want them to do and what follows is a clash of wills. This is not the relationship the Father desires. He is after our hearts and us delighting in doing his will.

Obedience is orphan hearted. What must I do to please God? Just as the disciples had grown up in a rules based system so too have we. Unbeknown to us we have swapped a life of freedom and an abundant life for one of servitude and restriction. The challenge of Jesus is to let that all go and leave it behind in order that we can step into our true freedom and identity as sons and daughters. What a change that is! When we really think about it how can we ever do enough to please the God of the universe? How can we ever win his favour by our good works? Well the good news is we don't need to because it's all been done for us. Jesus is the way, we are taken with him to the Father where we can experience a new freedom as we discover our true identity, one which has been lost for far too long.

Here we have two strong forces clashing powerfully. The force that won in the garden and led mankind down the empty, barren path of being fatherless is about to be shattered by a life-changing truth. A truth which never left the heart of the Father and which he has carried for all those years is about to be revealed. A force that led us away from the heart and presence of the Father is being confronted head-on. The wrong is being put right. One sentence is all it takes to reverse our destiny. Yes, Jesus said it to his disciples but those words echo through all of history and resonate into our hearts today.

In this one sentence Jesus reverses the battle which started in the garden. This is a life changing moment, this is the point in history when everything changes.

"I will not leave you as orphans, I will come to you".

This is the declaration of hope and restoration that is made over your life and my life. No longer do we need to live in turmoil and have troubled hearts. No longer are we lost with that empty, restless heart within us. No longer are we sentenced to independence and self-sufficiency. We are brought to the Father and the emptiness of our heart is dealt with by the unstoppable transforming power of love.

This is a cry that has to have a personal impact in each of our hearts. It requires an individual response. It invites us to turn away from the empty orphan hearted ways in which we have lived.

Dare I say it, many good Christians will go to Heaven and only step into their sonship as they enter their eternal inheritance. Brothers and sisters this is for us, it is for us now. This great confrontation can put an end to our orphan ways and set us free, enabling us to turn and step into the glorious freedom of living as sons and daughters. Jesus reverses everything as he declares over you and me "I will not leave fatherless and in a kingdom of fear, I will come to you and I will Father you". We can live as Jesus lived; this is what John means when he says we can walk as Jesus walked (1 John 2:6).

As **we** live as sons and daughters to the Father I believe those famous words will resonate through our lives. Those around us will see a change in us, they will see (although they may not be able to express it in words) the orphan hearted ways fall from us. As we live this life of sonship and live loved those words "I will not leave you as orphans, I will come to you" will be spoken through our actions and our love-filled heart. Our lives will be used to bring freedom to captive and broken hearts as we too will be able to point orphans to their Father and in doing so we will help to lead them home.

When Jesus spoke those words it was the moment in history when he lifted the blanket of depression that had fallen onto the human heart. This is not just a clash of cultures or ideologies, it is a clash of two kingdoms. In the garden the kingdom of fear won but now the kingdom of love conquers as Jesus declares that we are free from our orphan ways.

Jesus started the chapter with the words "*do not let your hearts be troubled*" and he ends in the same way: "*Peace I leave with you; my peace I give you. I do not give to you as the world gives. Do not let your hearts be troubled and do not be afraid*" (John 14:27).

This clash between two kingdoms shows us the depth of the Father's love. We have lived like Cain, restless wanderers on the face of the earth. Our hearts are in turmoil and distress as we live outside of the perfect contentment which can only be found as we make our home with Father. Jesus comes to bring peace and rest as he announces that our restless wandering is over. No longer do we need to live as orphans but we are brought into a family which we will belong to forever. Jesus takes you and me to the Father in order that we can discover our true home.

Our orphan ways are over when we recognise that we are the beloved. The discovery that we belong and that we are at home with the Father is the key for our troubled hearts finding rest and peace.

As Jesus redeems us from our orphan ways we are put back on the path God originally intended for us, the path of sonship. To seal our redemption, Jesus promises to send the Holy Spirit who will be another Comforter or Helper. He will always be with us and will continually remind us of all that Jesus has done for us. Jesus brings peace to troubled hearts and he wants us to continue living in that peace. To do so we need to receive comfort, which enables us to live from a nurtured heart, and this is something we will explore together in the next chapter.

The great confrontation is between a Son (Jesus) and an orphan (Satan). This time the Son wins and in doing so we are liberated. The desire of the Father's heart is now fully satisfied as sons and daughters can come home.

Chapter 5

Comfort

There are many expressions of love but unfortunately, in this area, the English language is lacking. The Sanskrit language has ninety-six words for love, ancient Persian has eighty and Greek has four. In English however, we only have one word for love and we expect it to convey a whole range of emotions and feelings. How do we know what someone means when they say "I love you?".

We typically refer to the Greek words for love when we are trying to be a bit more descriptive but even they do not give as full a picture as we sometimes need.

Agape is the self-less, unconditional love of God which is ultimately expressed in him sending Jesus to redeem us and turn our hearts back to him. In fact, contained within agape love are all the other expressions of the Father's love simply because God is love (1 John 4:8). *Eros* is the romantic or sexual love which has sadly been used in modern culture to pollute or distort what true love is meant to be. *Phileo* love is brotherly or family affection, a love which says "I like you". It is this word that Jesus uses in John 16:27 when he says "the Father himself loves you" what he is really saying is the Father likes us! He does not love us because something uncontrollable takes over his personality, he loves us because **he is love** and he actually enjoys our company.

There is another word for love which is *storge* and this depicts a close bond of familial love most acutely demonstrated by mothers. It is a deep nurturing love that envelops us and makes us feel safe.

There is one expression of love which I now want to explore and that is comfort. Comfort is perhaps a combination of the loves referred to above but in particular it is an expression of love which goes to the core of deep pain. Let's start off by looking at the dictionary definition of comfort as this is very enlightening.

Comfort: *to bring relief from pain, distress or affliction, to satisfy, to strengthen within. To provide a sense of wellbeing. Quiet enjoyment.*

When we are emotionally empty we need comfort. When we are in shock we need comfort. Whenever we feel alone, abandoned, in pain, sick, wounded, broken, bereaved, rejected – we need to experience comfort. The amount of comfort we need has to go beyond and exceed the pain or wound which we have experienced. Every trauma however big or small has to be met with a greater level of comfort. To bring healing and wholeness the comfort we need has to be greater than the original source of pain. If we do not receive this we are left in pain or discomfort.

It's a bit like a container; all of the trauma has to be removed and then replaced with love and comfort. If any trauma remains buried in our heart then the comfort we've received simply floats on top and all the while there is that nagging feeling of pain, or discomfort, which eats away at our heart. Comfort reaches down into the depths of our heart and goes underneath the pain so it is the pain which floats up and then can be skimmed away. Comfort has to go beneath the pain in order to wash it away and leave a heart which is nurtured and at rest.

A quick look at my electronic concordance showed me how important comfort is to God. Comfort (or the Comforter) is mentioned eighty-three times in the English Standard Version, seventy-two times in the New International Version and one hundred and nineteen times in the King James Version. It is clearly an important topic to God and, as we saw in the previous chapter, one that Jesus addressed when he confronted our orphan ways. Some translations even translate John 14:18 as "I will not leave you comfortless". Living an orphan hearted life is where we are not comforted or nurtured and instead of having someone to look after us we have had to look after ourselves and make sure that we are the answer to all our needs.

Before we look at comfort in more detail let's take a brief look at the opposite, for it is a tragic existence. Being comfortless means we are left in a broken state of despair and despair is hopeless. Time Magazine published an article several years ago on the despair of the super-rich, those with more money than they could ever spend but inside they were hopeless, filled with despair and despondency. I came across this very telling quote about hopelessness: "You've gotta have hope. Without hope life is *meaningless. Without hope life is meaning less and less.*" When we are not comforted it is easy to lose hope!

Solomon put into words the desperate state of the uncomforted heart:

"*Again, I observed all the oppression that takes place under the sun. I saw the tears of the oppressed, with no one to comfort them. The oppressors have great power, and there was no-one to comfort them. So I concluded that the dead are better off than the living. But most fortunate of all are those who are not yet born. For they have not seen all the evil that is done under the sun.*" (*Ecclesiastes 4:1-3 NLT*)

This is a stark warning. It is better to be dead or never to be born at all than to be without comfort. I hope you are beginning to see why this is such an important topic.

King David knew what comfort was. We don't know everything about his background but we do know his father 'forgot' to include him in the family line-up when Samuel came to choose the next king. We know that King Saul rejected him and tried to kill him on several occasions. When he took food to his brothers on the battle field they looked down on him and teased his youth and smallness, I wonder if their opinion changed when they watched him slay Goliath? It does seem as if David had suffered a lot of rejection and maybe was misunderstood as he was probably a lot more sensitive in nature than his warrior brothers.

Despite the rejection David understood what true comfort was. He found it in the heart of his Heavenly Father. He experienced a deep satisfaction in his heart; for him, "it was truly well with his soul". Maybe as he sat out in the hills with the sheep, singing some of his Psalms, that the Father came to him and poured comforting love into his heart. After killing lions and bears and feeling the stress and adrenaline rush maybe he experienced a deep comfort in his heart which enabled him to write verses such as:

"My heart is not proud, O LORD, my eyes are not haughty; I do not concern myself with great matters or things too wonderful for me. But I have calmed and quieted myself, I am like a weaned child with its mother; like a weaned child I am content." (Psalm 131:1-2)

"May your unfailing love be my comfort, according to your promise to your servant."
(Psalm 119:76)

"Hear my voice when I call, O LORD; be merciful to me and answer me. Though my father and mother forsake me, the LORD will receive me." (Psalm 27:7&10)

"Even though I walk through the darkest valley, I will fear no evil, for you are with me; your rod and your staff, they comfort me." (Psalm 23:4)

The Father's love will always comfort us.

"Therefore if you have any encouragement from being united with Christ, if any comfort from his love, if any common sharing in the Spirit, if any tenderness and compassion, then make my joy complete by being like-minded, having the same love, being one in spirit and of one mind." (Philippians 2:1-2)

If we do not open our hearts to receive the comforting love of the Father in areas where we need it, we will seek comfort in other areas. Whilst we seek comfort, what we will end up receiving are false comforts such as: controlling or destructive relationships, sex, pornography, shopping, possessions, alcohol, well…anything really. They are false comforts and whilst they may dampen the pain they will always leave us coming back for more.

Love provides true comfort and the quality of love we have received determines the comfort we have received. However good our parents have been they could only pass on the love they themselves had received. At best, all of us have only ever received partial and incomplete love and therefore we have not received the comfort we've really needed. This is why we need to keep coming back to the source and allow our Heavenly Father to comfort us with his perfect and complete love. Often times we have been the recipient of a love which has been manipulative or controlling – the Father's love is not like that, it is a giving love.

The prophet Isaiah shows us how and when we can receive comfort. He shows us the importance and magnitude of this amazing gift which is given to us even when we rebel or wander off on our own way.

We can receive comfort when we are afflicted or in a state of distress. Even if we have caused the affliction ourselves there is always redemption and restoration.

"Comfort, comfort my people, says your God. Speak tenderly to Jerusalem, and proclaim to her that her hard service has been completed, that her sin has been paid for, that she has received from the LORD's hand double for all her sins." (Isaiah 40:1-2)

Comfort will transform the dry and barren places in our heart and give us joy and gladness. Instead of being in sorrow we can recover a thankful heart.

"The LORD will surely comfort Zion and will look with compassion on all her ruins; he will make her deserts like Eden, her wastelands like the garden of the LORD. Joy and gladness will be found in her, thanksgiving and the sound of singing." (Isaiah 51:3)

When we mourn, for whatever reason, we need to be comforted and as we are that comfort begins to replace the trauma we've been through. When we've lost a loved one I know the pain is very real and deep but what I'm conveying, though sounding simple, is an ongoing process of being comforted so that over time we receive our healing and relief from the acute pain we've experienced.

"....to proclaim the year of the LORD's favour, and the day of vengeance of our God; to comfort all who mourn;" (Isaiah 61:2)

"As a mother comforts her child, so will I comfort you; and you will be comforted over Jerusalem." (Isaiah 66:13)

We have already seen how Jesus refers to 'another Comforter' in John 14 which clearly implies that he was one too. He took a disparate group of young men and over a three year period transformed them into the people we see and follow throughout the book of Acts. He took Simon the Zealot, who would have hated the Romans, and put him to work with the Matthew, the tax collector, the guy who worked for the Romans and cheated his fellow countrymen. After Lazarus had died we read that Jesus wept, he felt the pain and loss of a good friend, and then he goes on to comfort the two sisters, Mary and Martha.

I imagine the disciples had become used to being comforted which is why Jesus re-assures them by sending another Comforter, the Spirit of Truth, who will be with them (and us) forever.

Jesus knows we need comfort, particularly when we have lost something which has been precious to us. In the Beatitudes we read:

"Blessed are those who mourn, for they will be comforted." (Matthew 5:4)

Or, as The Message puts it:

"You're blessed when you feel you've lost what is most dear to you. Only then can you be embraced by the One most dear to you."

When Jesus fed the five thousand he was not simply engaging in an administrative obligation but he was genuinely concerned about the people's needs. He wanted them fed before they journeyed home. His story of the lost sheep is one of concern for something of value which has been lost and which he wants to see found again. This story mirrors Isaiah 40:11 where we read how God longs to hold us close to his heart, just as a shepherd carries a lamb. This is the comforting heart of the Father demonstrated through the life of his son, Jesus.

When we receive comfort we become connected to the source of comfort. Comfort takes away our disconnectedness and feelings of abandonment. Jesus promises us another Comforter. He declares our orphan ways are over and then he draws us into this intimate relationship where we know we are loved by the Father and where we know we have found our home. (John 14:19-23)

This is the fruit of comfort.

Paul, too, discovered the power of comfort.

"Praise be to the God and Father of our Lord Jesus Christ, the Father of compassion and the God of all comfort, who comforts us in all our troubles, so that we can comfort those in any trouble with the comfort we ourselves receive from God. For just as we share abundantly in the sufferings of Christ, so also our comfort abounds through Christ. If we are distressed, it is for your comfort and salvation; if we are comforted, it is for your comfort, which produces in you patient endurance of the same sufferings we suffer. And our hope for you is firm, because we know that just as you share in our sufferings, so also you share in our comfort." (2 Corinthians 1:3-7)

What had Paul been through that enabled him to write this? He had discovered through all his tribulations that God was the God of **all** comfort who would comfort him in **all** his troubles. That's a pretty complete description of comfort.

Whatever trauma or pain we have been through we need to be comforted by the love of the Father. He really is enough. For every feeling of aloneness, abandonment, brokenness or bereavement we need to be comforted. Our Father is the source of ALL comfort. I vividly remember witnessing a horrific road accident in Uganda, thankfully we were all ok but around us was carnage. It was traumatic to say the least and then there was the dawning realisation that no ambulances would arrive nor was there any State emergency medical care, it was all down to the families to arrive and take care of their loved ones. After witnessing that we needed comfort!

It is only as we receive comfort that we are able to comfort others. There is a big difference between sympathy and comfort and whilst sympathy is good in itself it does not go to the depths that comfort reaches. Sympathy may do the other person some good, it shows you care and it's maybe all you can do at the time, but comfort goes deeper. If we have been comforted we can impart the comfort we have received to others (note, as Paul says, it is not our own comfort).

As we receive comfort, Paul writes, we are able to endure our suffering. Yes, we will suffer and that suffering may not be taken away but Father's divine answer is for us to receive and live in this deep expression of love, which is comfort.

This is the depth of the Father's love for us. He wants us to be comforted. He does not want the trauma to remain in our heart where it will continue to cause pain and discomfort. He wants the power of his love to come under that pain and to be the source of it being taken out of our heart. He truly is the Father of compassion and the God of all comfort.

Chapter 6

Peace

In chapter 4 I highlighted the aim and purpose of Jesus' ministry in which he clearly shows us we are no longer orphans but are sons and daughters. For us, the application of this great confrontation is that we can leave behind orphan hearted Christianity and begin to discover the absolute truth and reality of the gospel. We are the Father's sons and daughters.

In John 14, Jesus ends with the words *"Peace I leave with you, my peace I give you. I do not give as the world gives. Do not let your hearts be troubled and do not be afraid"* (John 14:27).

As we live in our sonship (which I believe is the true expression of Christianity) we will step into and live in peace. A peace that is not defined by worldly standards or conditions but an inner peace, which is a gift. Peace is the fruit of the Holy Spirit living within us, it is a seed that is planted and which grows within us. The peace Jesus is talking about is not something we can drum up or create by ensuring all our external circumstances are in good order. Of course, it is true that some people are more peaceful than others, that some homes are more restful and some places more calming and gentle. How many of us love to walk in the countryside enjoying the peace and beauty of our Father's creation? Some (and I'm not one of them) can find peace in the centre of a busy, bustling city. Some people are inevitably more laid back and less stressful to be with than others. All of these things are true but they are not the peace that Jesus is talking about.

There are two stories in the Gospels which demonstrate the peace Jesus lives in and these are when he was fast asleep in the boat and secondly, when he walked out on the water to the disciples. In both stories, the disciples are setting off in their boat across the sea of Galilee. In the first story Jesus is with them and after a hard day's work he has fallen asleep. Not even the fury of the storm woke him, yet, at the same time, the disciples were fearing for their lives. In desperation they wake Jesus who simply looks around him and says, "Quiet! Be still!"; that's all it took! Instantly the storm stopped and the sea became totally calm.

In the midst of a storm Jesus was at peace. This is a picture of how our hearts can be when we have discovered that our true home is with the Father, we can be at peace irrespective of what is going on around us. When we are centred on him, trusting and dependent on our Father, we will live in peace. Whatever is going on around us does not need to shape or condition the state of our heart. We do not need to swing backwards and forwards, tossed by the external events of our lives. These things are very real and are things we have to walk through but they do not need to be the barometer of our heart. When we have experienced our homecoming into Father's arms his love becomes the source of peace in our hearts. Peace is an internal force not governed by external circumstances. James Jordan says: "You can never still a storm you can't sleep through".

The second story is of the disciples going ahead of Jesus to Bethsaida after the feeding of the five thousand. Jesus has dismissed the people and then he goes up the mountain to pray. As he looks out across the lake he sees his disciples struggling as the wind was against them. You have to be physically strong to row against a storm and the disciples did not have the strength on this occasion. Jesus walks out to them on the water and, having climbed into the boat, he calms the storm.

Like the disciples, our own strength is not enough. There are times when it feels as if we are rowing single-handed against the storm. We are not making any headway, in fact we have been blown backwards by the storm that engulfs us. Storms come in varying shapes and sizes: financial, health, emotional, family needs or just the 'stuff of life'. How often do we become aware that our strength is simply not enough; on our own we can't make any headway or progress. All our hard work and effort does not take us anywhere.

Thankfully we have a Saviour. Jesus sees our struggles and he comes to us. He comes into the place where we, in ourselves, are losing the battle and he calms our storm. As his presence fills our situation peace comes. Why? Because he is the Prince of Peace. He brings his peace into our lives and this peace goes beyond our understanding.

These stories are very familiar and they paint two slightly different pictures. Jesus is always with us in our troubles and secondly he sees us in trouble and comes to us. Both are equally true. He is always with us and wants his peace to fill our hearts. But he also recognises that there are times, for whatever reasons, that we are trying to row against the storm in our own strength and then he comes to us. Either way he is the Prince of Peace and he wants to impart that peace, his peace, into our hearts.

The peace we receive as we leave our orphan hearted ways behind is one that brings our hearts to a place of rest and contentment. It causes the striving of our heart to cease as we learn to trust our heavenly Father. As Jesus says in Matthew 11 it is a journey for those with childlike hearts, we are invited to respond and come as Jesus reveals the Father to us.

"So everyone, come to me! Are you weary, carrying a heavy burden? Then come to me. I will refresh your life for I am your Oasis. Simply join your life with mine. Learn my ways and you'll discover that I'm gentle, humble, easy to please. You will find refreshment and rest in me." (Matthew 11:28-29 TPT).

He is our Oasis of peace and he offers us a pathway which is both pleasant to walk and a burden which is light.

Peace has always been at the centre of God's heart for his people. Peace was a foundation stone for the people of Israel. When Yahweh, the Almighty God, was your king and your Father, living in peace should have been an automatic quality of life. The contentment of knowing God was your provider should have been overwhelming. Yet despite all this the people chose the path of independence wanting their own king and their own way of doing things. God does not give up on their unfaithfulness as, in the centre of the law, is the famous Aaronic blessing:

"The Lord bless you and keep you; the Lord make his face shine upon you and be gracious to you; the Lord turn his face towards you and give you peace". (Numbers 6:24-26)

That blessing can be real for us as well. The Father longs to bless, to shine his glory upon us and cause us to walk in his peace. Not a peace of our own making but his peace. Living in love keeps us in that perfect peace.

"You will keep in perfect peace him whose mind is steadfast, because he trusts in you." (Isaiah 26:3)

His peace restores our soul, it strengthens and refreshes us. Psalm 23 is psalm of peace. Despite all the turmoil around us he provides a place of peace and security where we can be at home. There is safety, refuge, provision and comfort for us when we find our home in him.

When we are at peace we are content. This is not just contentment on the surface it is deep within our hearts. It is a contentment which will start to govern our whole personality as it becomes the hallmark of our life. Paul writes that peace will rule in our hearts (Colossians 3:15) and that the Father's peace will guard our hearts and minds (Philippians 4:7). Peace, though gentle, is a powerful force that really can and will change us.

Jesus, after the resurrection and as he ends his earthly life, comes to his disciples and twice says to them, "Peace be with you". He then breathes upon them so they may receive the Holy Spirit, the new Comforter who will always be with them and who will fill their hearts with peace.

Again let me stress this peace is not of our own making. It is the fruit of the Holy Spirit dwelling within us. It is a seed planted in us that grows to govern our life from the inner place of our heart. It is a God given gift growing in our heart.

Horatio Spafford was a wealthy lawyer who had a large property portfolio in Chicago. He had a son, four daughters and a beautiful wife. Humanly speaking he had it made. But at the very height of his professional and financial success his young son died from scarlet fever and then, in October 1871, the great Chicago Fire destroyed every one of his properties. In order to recover from this tragedy Spafford booked an ocean going liner for a trip to Europe. At the last minute Spafford had to stay in Chicago to deal with some business so his wife and daughters went on ahead. Tragedy stuck on the voyage as the Spafford's boat collided with another ship and all four daughters were drowned; only his wife, Anna, survived.

A few days later Spafford took another boat to England so he could be with his wife. It was on that trip that he wrote the now famous hymn:

When peace, like a river, attended my way,
When sorrows like sea billows roll
Whatever my lot, Thou hast taught me to say
It is well, it is well with my soul.

The following verse recounts Spafford's unyielding faith in God, his assurance of his salvation and his knowledge that whatever happens peace can fill his heart.

For me, be it Christ, be it Christ hence to live
If Jordan above me shall roll,
No pang shall be mine, for in death as in life
Thou wilt whisper thy peace to my soul.

It is well, it is well with my soul.

We can only begin to imagine the encounter he'd had with the Presence of God that enabled him to write those words so soon after experiencing that much tragedy. The sorrow and sadness was washed away when peace flowed into his heart and life. Spafford came to a place in the midst of heartache and pain where he could truly say "it is well, it is well with my soul". Those words continue to inspire and comfort today.

Such peace is not rational, it is not dependent on our circumstances but it is a divine impartation into hearts. It is not based on our feelings but it is a result of the Spirit of Sonship within us. When everything is going against us we can be at peace because it is not our peace but his peace. When our mind wants to go off in one direction (normally towards fear) peace will take us in the opposite one. When our emotions go one way, peace takes us the other.

Most of Paul's letters either begin or end with the words "grace and peace to you". Whatever the content of his letters, Paul has a pastoral heart and wants his readers to dwell in peace. It's like he is doing what Jesus did when he breathed his peace into the disciples. Paul wants the same for his readers and therefore for us as well. All too often we skip the first and last verses of these letters as they are only an introduction or a final greeting. We pass them by as we don't think they have much 'content'. I urge you to read them and as you read the words "grace and peace", take a deep breath and breathe in the peace which Paul offers. Let it soak into your heart and spirit.

We read in Galatians 5 that the fruit of the Spirit is love, joy, peace, patience, kindness, goodness, faithfulness, gentleness and self-control (Galatians 5: 22-23). The law does not stand against these qualities for they are the result of a life lived in love. Jesus lived his life in perfect and complete love, perfect and complete joy, perfect and complete peace and so on. As the Spirit of Sonship dwells in our hearts this fruit will grow within us as well. Love, joy, peace and so on will grow and mature in us as we begin to live the life of the beloved. A practical expression of the Father's love being poured into our hearts will be us living in a level of peace that goes beyond our understanding. Peace can become the hallmark of our lives and a beacon of hope to others who desperately long for contentment in their hearts.

Isaiah tells us that God's ways are not our ways; in fact they are totally different. We see occasional glimpses of what his ways are like but we will never fully fathom them. If we think we have, all we have done is minimised them and made them too small. We can never fully work God out. And this is why we require faith. Faith is the ability to see beyond ourselves and to believe that all we hope for can happen. It is pulling God's future into our present as we put our dependence and trust in him. It is knowing that he cares for us because he loves us and that he will provide for us and look after us no matter what. It is the gift of faith which enables the striving of our heart to cease and, as it does, his peace will take over and lead us into our promised rest. It is our faith in him which allows the words from Isaiah to be fulfilled: *"you will go out in joy and be led forth in peace, the mountains and hills will burst into singing before you and all the trees of the field will clap their hands"* (Isaiah 55:12).

This is the depth of the Father's love for us. He is totally content. Even with all of the problems of the world, the cares and needs of seven and a half billion people he is totally content. He is at peace. Our Father wants us to share that peace with him so we too find a place of contentment where our hearts are at rest and at peace. When nations live at peace the population of the country is healthier. When we have the same peace in our hearts as Horatio Spafford experienced, we will feel the effects throughout our body. Conversely if we are at war with ourselves the effects of that dis-peace in our hearts will be felt throughout our body.

The Father wants us to live in peace. His love and care for us is expressed through this gift of peace that enables us to walk as Jesus walked. Peace, like comfort, sets our hearts free and leads us further along the path of love knowing we have come home to the Father.

My prayer as you read this, is that peace like a river will fill your heart. That the striving and busyness of your heart will cease and you, like Horatio Spafford, will be able to say "it is well, it is well with my soul".

"The fruit of the Holy Spirit within you is divine love in all its various expressions. This love is revealed through: joy that overflows, peace that subdues, patience that endures, kindness on display, a life full of virtue, faith that prevails, gentleness of heart and strength of spirit. Never set the law above these qualities, for they are meant to be limitless." (Galatians 6:22-23 TPT)

Chapter 7

"We Get to Live This Life"

My good friend, Helene King, who is well into her seventies and still travelling the world, sharing and imparting the love of the Father loves to say this; "we get to live this life". Normally there is a twinkle in her eye and a smile on her face as she says it, very often when we are sitting together in an airport lounge on our way home from another school or conference. Helene understands something we all need to understand and that is the words of Jesus in John 10:10 "*the thief comes only to steal and kill and destroy; I have come that they may have life and have it to the full*". The Passion Translation puts it like this: "*A thief has only one thing in mind, he wants to steal, kill and destroy. But my desire is to give you everything in abundance, more than you expect, life in its fullness until you overflow.*"

It's a verse we quote often but I wonder if we fully understand what the implications of that statement are for us. What does life to the full really mean? How do we get it? And how do we keep it? The problem is we spend so long guarding ourselves against the thief who is trying to steal and destroy that we do not turn the other way and see the life that can be enjoyed to the full. We miss out on our abundant life because we have been distracted and have lapsed into protectionist mode. We miss out on the gift of being able to "live freely and lightly" (Matthew 11:30 The Message).

We have made a mistake and fallen into a trap. When we talk about a full, or an abundant life we limit it to what we call our 'Christian life'. People talk about wanting to enjoy their Christian life and we all nod our heads in agreement. But what does it mean? I used to quite like the statement "I really want to enjoy my Christian life", I believed it, I longed for it and thought it was a good thing until I started to think about what the words really said. In fact, the more I thought about it the more I realised it was what it did not say that could be more important.

Take a moment and ask yourself "what is your Christian life?" Is it when you are in church? Going to your mid-week meeting? Enjoying worship or simply spending some quiet time with God? If that is your Christian life what label do you put on the rest of your life? Are you any less Christian when you are in the office, doing the shopping, enjoying some recreation or doing the dishes? We have created this ridiculous spiritual versus secular divide where one is good (even holy) and the other is bad (and verging on being sinful). It is totally ludicrous and completely unbiblical. There is no such divide in the heart of the Father. How many of you parents separate your children's lives into what they do for a living and what they do when you are together as a family. Of course you don't; they are always your son or daughter. This is how the Father sees us, as sons and daughters, he does not divide us into Christian and well, what would you call the other part of your life?

When we stand back and look at it we realise we don't turn on being a Christian at certain times or for certain activities. Once we are born again we are a Christian irrespective of the varying activities we do at different times. Our 'Christian life' encompasses everything. If we place a higher value on some of the things we do and think they are more worthy this is wrong thinking and a false assumption. In fact, such attitudes create a hierarchy and therefore division in the church. Those who lead worship are more spiritual than those who do the chairs or make the coffee - I don't think so!

What we end up doing is playing a game we may as well call "Christian schizophrenia". We think we can change our identity and therefore our value or acceptance before God. It's a game with not much fun and certainly no merit attached to it.

This mistake has meant we have limited the words of Jesus and only consider that this abundant life affects a few areas of our lives. Jesus did not say he came to make us happy in church, he came that we might have life (all of life) to the full. Abundant life in every area. This may come as a surprise to you but you are allowed to enjoy everything you do.

Now I am not talking about us being free to enjoy the pleasures of sin, nor am I saying we can do as we please. When we love our heavenly Father we will want to live like Jesus and do those things that please him. We will want to walk away from sin because we know it creates a barrier or a distance between us. We will value an open heart of love above dutiful sacrifices or offerings, we will delight in doing his will (Psalm 40).

If one mistake has been to create a spiritual/secular divide another has been to misinterpret the law of the Old Testament. Maybe even the word 'law' conjures up the wrong meaning, after all a law is something we have to work hard to obey. Failure to obey the law leads to a penalty.

When we understand that the Old Testament law and, more specifically, the ten commandments were given to be a glimpse into the personality and nature of God we start to see things in a different light. They are picture to us of God's character rather than being a legalistic set of rules. So, for example, "thou shalt not steal" is a glimpse into the nature of God where he says "there is nothing in me that would ever steal so if you want to be like me you won't steal either". "Thou shall not commit adultery" shows us there is nothing in the nature and personality of God that would ever want a broken, painful relationship. If we are like him then there will be nothing in us that goes after broken, destructive relationships.

We have turned the nature and personality of a loving Father into a set of rules, a list of 'thou shalts' and 'thou shalt nots'. The law has stopped being a gateway into the heart of the perfect Father and has become a framework for man trying to please God and win his favour through activity or behaviour. An impossible task but one that continues to consume us and take a vast amount of our emotional energy. We can never win God's approval through our own endeavours; it doesn't work that way.

I do believe there is a price to pay, I do believe there are sacrifices we have to make. But I also firmly believe we have got things in the wrong order. We have put the sacrifice or price first in the hope that they in themselves will be enough to buy the relevant ticket. The ticket to where or what we're not quite sure, but we feel as if we have to buy our own salvation or redemption. It is actually the other way round. Sacrifice comes out of the heart filled with love. Something happens in our hearts which cannot stop us wholeheartedly following the lover of our soul. In finding love and coming home we have found that pearl of great price which is worth everything. Pursuing love is the thing that will cause us to give up everything else, however valuable those things are, and go with our heavenly Father on this journey into love and life.

Jesus met a rich young man and asked him if he could give everything away in order to inherit eternal life. This young man had kept all of the law, he'd done all the right things but he had something in his life that was more important to him than the life Jesus offered. Maybe his heart was so tied up with his possessions that he was unable to receive love.

We have misinterpreted the law and that continues to colour our view of the pathway to God. Singing the Sunday School song "I have decided to follow Jesus" reinforces this; that it is my choice and my decision to follow him. It's a song with a nice sentiment but it puts the onus on us and completely negates his love which searches us out and draws us to him. He conceived us before the beginning of time and because he knows us so intimately we can begin to believe that he has always been our Father. We can begin to believe that because he knows us, he also loves us and if he loves us then maybe we can begin to experience that love being poured into our hearts (Romans 5:5). We do not make a way to God. Jesus is the way to the Father and as we have already seen, he longs to reveal the Father to us. He goes on revealing the Father to us.

Throughout the Old Testament there were a few people who went beyond the legalistic framework of the law and had a personal relationship with God. Noah, Abraham, Moses, David, Isaiah and Jeremiah to name a few. They knew who God was and experienced his Father's love, which enabled them to point the way to the coming of Jesus and the redemption of mankind. They could see an end to the orphan hearted ways mankind had stepped into and which were a consequence of the trap Satan had set for Adam and Eve.

Others continued to live in fear of God and that fear did what fear always does. It paralysed them. Jonah could never quite trust the goodness and love of God and, although he'd experienced it himself, he could not let God show the same love and mercy to the city of Nineveh. Gideon struggled to believe the goodness of God but eventually he overcame his fear as he learned to trust in that same goodness. Characters like Jonah and Gideon give us hope as we too can be like them when fear takes a hold of us. The good news is that perfect love always casts out fear. Fear paralyses, but love always liberates. The more we live in love the more freedom we will enjoy as the fear within us is driven out.

When fear rules we allow ourselves to be seduced by the tree of the knowledge of good and evil. We therefore choose to decide what is right and what is wrong, what is good for us and what is bad. It ceases to be a journey of love where we give ourselves freely to the loving direction and care of our Father, but rather it becomes our assessment of what we need to do in order to please God and win his favour. So the eyes and ears of our heart remain closed. Instead of responding to love we try to keep ourselves within the 'safe' framework of the law, our law!

One of my favourite Old Testament stories is that of Ruth. It's a love story between a man and woman, between a rich man and a poor migrant worker who has been brought to the land seeking better things. It's a story of commitment and loyalty between Ruth and her mother-in-law, Naomi. It's a story of human love and kindness but it also portrays the depth of the Father's love for his children. We see, and feel, that depth of redeeming love and compassion. Through this beautiful story we get a glimpse of what full and abundant life is really like. The story of Boaz and Ruth is one of provision, safety, security, relationship and inheritance. Ruth is brought into a family where her past does not matter. She's accepted for who she is, her nationality and background are completely irrelevant to Boaz as he showers his love upon her. Ruth is redeemed and given back everything that Naomi and her husband had lost all those years before.

Not only do we see the full life which Ruth enters into, we also see this same redemption coming to Naomi. She freely gives Ruth to Boaz, thinking only of the younger woman's good and future. She puts Ruth above herself, not for any reward, but for Ruth's future prosperity and security. In turn she too receives an inheritance and security for her own future.

Just as Boaz's redeeming love brought Ruth into a safe and secure place where she was loved and cared for, so the Father's redeeming love brings us into a wide open space where our hearts can be free. His love brings us to a place where we know we are part of a family, where our past does not matter and where we can be accepted for who we are. His love brings us home. This is the depth of the Father's love.

To fully experience this we need the eyes of our heart to be opened so we can know "the hope to which we have been called" (Ephesians

1:18). This hope and calling is to a family were God is our Father, where we daily experience him being a Father to us.

Jesus tells us that eternal life is knowing the Father and the one he has sent (John 17:3). Our eternal life began the moment we were born again and it is this eternal life that the Father wants us to enjoy to the full. It is this eternal life which is meant to be an abundant one. This encompasses all of our activities and all of the things we invest our time and energy into. It is not meant to represent only a segment of who we are or what we do. It covers everything we do and everything we are.

Like Ruth we are brought to a safe place where we are loved no matter what. We are provided for, we are cared for, all we need comes from our loving Heavenly Father. No longer do we need to strive to win his favour or work hard to please him. We can have a childlike trust and dependency in our Father simply knowing and resting on his goodness and kindness.

This is the depth of the Father's love.

We really do get to live this life!

Chapter 8

A Season of Shaking

There are times in our life when we are drawn into the depth of his love in a greater way. It's not that he loves us more intensely but rather we are drawn into a greater reliance and dependency on him and his love for us. All of us at some time or another will go through a season of shaking; it may be part of our personal journey, our family journey, our ministry or church life or even part of the changes affecting our country.

Our natural reaction is to try and run from the uncertainty that change brings in order that we might re-discover a safe haven. Change is unnerving and unsettles us because we have become familiar with what we accept as 'normal'. As things are shaken and change looms on our horizon there is only one truly safe place and that is to run into the arms of love and allow ourselves to be carried by the One who has the eternal perspective. Our own view is often too restrictive and can limit what Father wants to do in our hearts.

The writer of Hebrews understands this when he says:

This phrase, "Yet once more," indicates the removal of things that are shaken—that is, **things that have been made** *- in order that the things that cannot be shaken may remain. Therefore let us be grateful for receiving a kingdom that cannot be shaken, and thus let us offer to God acceptable worship, with reverence and awe, for our God is a consuming fire. (Hebrews 12:27-29)*

A time of change is often a season when things are shaken. This is not necessarily bad for us as it sorts out the wheat from the chaff, the God-made from the man-made, relationship from religion and the eternal from the temporary. It is a time when the things we have relied on or created in our own strength can fall away in order that we may begin to trust on the things which Father considers more important.

We fear change. However I believe we can face it with faith and an assurance that the door which is opening for us is better than the place we are leaving behind.

I am writing this shortly after the UK's 2016 referendum on EU membership and shortly before the US presidential election. Don't worry I am not about to become political; I know as many people who voted 'Remain' as voted 'Leave'. Everyone did so after examining the issues carefully, seeking to follow their conscience and above all prayerfully considering the options. I have friends with very passionate views on both side of the debate in the US. The point is we live in a time of great change and we can choose how we respond to it.

Are we going to respond to these seasons of shaking with fear or with faith?

Let's take some time to explore our experience of love as we face and go through times of change or seasons when it appears as if everything is being shaken.

John the Baptist describes Jesus coming to gather the wheat into the barn and to burn the resultant chaff (Matthew 3:12). This is a separation of what is holy, real and genuine from what is pretence or false. It is the challenge of religion and the emergence of a family. John's coming (and therefore that of Jesus) needs to be set in the context of Malachi 4 and Joel 2 which is the prophetic revelation of sons and daughters. It is the replacement of religion with relationship and the revelation of God's eternal heart to show himself as Father.

If we are living in the spirit of sonship change should not threaten us. As sons and daughters we have the security of knowing that Almighty God just happens to be our Father and he holds **everything** in his hand. Nothing takes him by surprise, he is not unsettled by any of the events in our life, in our family or in our nation. As sons and daughters we are gathered into that safe place and held 'in Christ'. Our home is with the Father.

Whenever there is a move of God the old or established ways are always threatened and the wineskin needs to change. Normally we ask ourselves the question "what should the wineskin be like" and this invariably leads us to create a structure. Too often we have sensed that God is doing something new and our response has been to create a structure to hold what we believe he is doing. That structure often limits what he wants to do as there is something so much bigger in his heart than we have in ours. Instead of trying to create a wineskin we should instead ask ourselves the question "what is the new wine". I believe we are living in a day when the Father is pouring his love into his children's hearts in order that we may know who he is and therefore who we are. This is the revelation we have been entrusted with. The new wine is his love poured into our hearts.

I do not believe this is purely for a season. We have had many moves of the Spirit, even in our lifetimes, and each one has waned with the church falling back into denominationalism and settling back into a religious form of duty and service. We have been refreshed for a season but the life has drained away as we have not had a container in which to hold it.

As the Father is being revealed, what we are experiencing now is the completion and fulfilment of the Trinity working together as one in the life of the church. As Father is revealed we become sons and daughters and so the true church is built. The foundation of this has to be love; firstly us being filled with his love and secondly us letting that love flow to a broken, hurting and wounded world.

He longs for purity and holiness. Our post-modern view of Christianity does not like these words as they have been taken out of context and portrayed as legalism. Purity and holiness are **not** legalism but they are the heart response of someone who values relationship. They are the response of a heart so filled with love that there is no desire to walk in a way which is ultimately in the opposite direction to where Father is leading. When we respond to love there will be nothing in our hearts that wants to walk in any other direction to the one that Father is leading us in.

Change comes in all shapes and sizes. We are shaken to varying degrees. It is all too easy to become discouraged or disillusioned and then we begin to lose heart.

In times of change it is the force of that change that rocks the foundation of our life. God may not cause the change but he uses it to let the chaff be blown away. He uses it to draw out the gold in our lives and let the wood, hay and stubble be consumed. He uses it to leave us purer and holier than we were before the season started. He uses it to take us deeper into him. He uses it to ensure that our lives are able to bear abundant and lasting fruit. He strips more of us away in order that more of him may be revealed.

A time of change is an opportunity to re-evaluate our core values. What are the things that matter? What are the things he has given us to do?

All too often, as time passes, we add things to our core values, maybe good ideas, maybe a slight deviation from the good works he has given us to do, maybe a broader path rather than the narrow one he first gave us. A time of shaking is an opportunity for those things to fall away so once again we can live in the purity of the revelation he has given to us. To centre ourselves on him.

Change is something we like to shy away from. We often say "change is here to stay" and there is an element of truth in that. We are encouraged to leave our 'comfort zone', to maintain a pioneer spirit and to pursue a vision. Yes, we need a vision, as Proverbs 29:18 reminds us without a vision we perish, or cast off restraint. Is it right, though, for us leave our comfort zone (whatever that means)?

As we are planted in love we are also planted in the Father's comfort. Comfort should become the mattress of our lives, the resting place of his love becoming the source and root of who we are. When comfort is the foundation of our hearts love will be dominant in these times of change.

It is interesting that the writer to the Hebrews says it will be the things that **are made** which will be removed through the shaking. Man made structures or responses will not stand as they do not have a firm foundation. The foundation for our lives is the Father's love and therefore anything not built on that will be shaken and if it has no roots it will be removed. The stronger and deeper our roots go into love the less likely it is that things will be uprooted and shaken out of our lives.

The kingdom of Heaven is a kingdom of love. It is not a kingdom of fear. When we live in fear we deny the power of love working in our lives and therefore we have a root system which is not secure. Fear will always lead us to look at the negatives, the what-ifs and the maybes. As we live in love so fear is driven out; the two can not exist side by side. When love comes, fear goes. If we build our lives on fear it is like the house built on sand and when the storms come (as they will) there are no foundations to hold the building up. When we build in love and on love we are like the house built on rock. The storms may come and lash against us but we are held by foundations that go down into the strongest force in the universe – the Father's love.

The kingdom of love cannot be shaken.

When we are rooted and grounded in love we live in an unshakeable kingdom which will guard us and keep us safe throughout the seasons of change. Living in love **will** produce the fruit of the Spirit in our lives. Joy, peace, patience, kindness, goodness, faithfulness, gentleness and self-control are the natural and automatic by-products of a life lived in love. When we live in love the Father's own Spirit living within us becomes our motivating force and the source of our life. We cannot survive the seasons of change in our own strength nor can we push through them with the power of our will alone. If our lives are governed by the law we will become desperate, worn out and discouraged. Relying on an old wineskin or an outdated religious mindset will not carry us through the seasons of change. It is only a life lived in love which will cause us to soar above our circumstances and enable us to journey through the season of change in rest and in peace.

This is the depth of love. Father's love embraces us and holds us through the seasons of change and the turmoil which they bring. Father's love sets us free even though the change may be painful. In a season when things are shaken our natural response may be to run and hide, hoping the season will pass quickly. Rather than hiding or pursuing our own independence let us run into the safe arms of love where we can be carried and embraced in the Father's perfect and complete love. Where we can rest in his perfect and complete comfort.

Chapter 9

Life in The Trinity

It seems to me that when we think about the persons of the Trinity we think about them in isolation from each other. We think about what Jesus can do for us, what the Holy Spirit can do for us and maybe even what the Father can do. We do not consider them as a single relational unit.

The problem is it is easier for us to consider what Jesus and the Holy Spirit can do for us because they have been more visibly present in our Christian experience. In the past the Father has been distant, angry or at best has acted through the other two members of the Trinity. All of which has led us to develop a mentality of the Godhead existing solely to satisfy our needs and desires.

Even in coming to Jesus and the Holy Spirit we are confused as to their respective roles and their individual personalities.

Jesus has become the person who heals us, provides for us, confirms our salvation and is the one we pray to. Although, in our prayers we often forget that he is our big brother and therefore we use a number of biblical titles when talking to him which has the natural effect of distancing him and de-personalising our relationship with him.

Jesus is the one who meets our needs and meets the needs of others. He is the mediator between our earthly life and our eternal inheritance (something we think we still have to earn).

Our historical view of Jesus fails to recognise who he is and what he has done for us – not only on the cross but also through his resurrection. Yes, he meets our needs, yes, he saves us but he can do so much more for each one of us. Yes, he looks in our direction but primarily he looks at his Father. Not only does he meet our needs and look 'man-ward' but he also introduces and releases the Holy Spirit into our lives.

This historical view of Jesus has created a need centred Christianity which has made our religion self centred rather than God (or Father) focussed.

The Pentecostal/Charismatic renewal has shifted this historical viewpoint but not in a way which is totally consistent with scripture.

The Holy Spirit, so long forgotten, is now welcomed into mainstream Christianity. The word "Pentecostal" describes the way in which the Holy Spirit has been introduced into the church. We have limited the person and influence of the Holy Spirit in a way that mirrors his appearance on the Day of Pentecost in Acts 2. On this occasion there was an outpouring of the Spirit, the fruit of which was men speaking in other tongues, a greater boldness and freedom than previously experienced. A freedom and an outpouring which led to a revival in which many were born again. That has become our paradigm for outpourings and manifestations of the Holy Spirit; but are we seeing revivals that produce the result described in John 15: abundant and lasting fruit?

Yes, this is what the Holy Spirit does and we need to welcome him with open hearts and enjoy such outpourings. But this is not all, there is more, much more to experience and enjoy.

In John 14 Jesus describes in great detail the role of the Holy Spirit and this is very different to our standard paradigm or perception. He is a person, he is a comforter (another comforter, therefore in addition to Jesus). He is a guide. Above all he comes to show us, to confirm to us and to bring alive in us that we are no longer orphans. If not orphans, then by definition we are sons and daughters. The Holy Spirit challenges the lie we believed in the garden; the lie that tells us we are fatherless.

Paul develops this further in both Romans and Galatians. As we receive the Spirit we are empowered, caused and even motivated to cry out "Abba, Father". Something in us comes alive when we receive the Spirit as our true identity begins to emerge and is confirmed within us. We know we are sons and daughters when the Spirit of **the** Son has been embedded in our hearts.

All of us are biological sons or daughters but that does not mean we live as a son or daughter. If our hearts are closed to our parents that knowledge purely describes a biological or legal fact. It does not describe a relationship. The Holy Spirit comes into our hearts and that changes everything. The Spirit of Sonship is the Spirit of both the Father and the Son and receiving the Holy Spirit changes our heart so that we know who He is and who we are!

Instead of describing a theoretical or legal relationship, instead of using terminology we start to live a relationship. Not as a clone or imitation of Jesus but we begin to live as he lived. We live as sons and daughters because we are sons and daughters.

It is an expression of life which flows from the gift of the Holy Spirit within us. It is much more than purely being enabled to do greater things, as vital and important as those things may be.

Too often we have viewed the Holy Spirit as the add-on enabler or fixer. A tool box full of goodies to help us in our Christian life, to make us more productive and maybe even make us better Christians.

Yes, the gifts of the Holy Spirit are important but they represent the "Pentecostal" expression of life. Focusing solely on these important and necessary gifts does not lead to us fully grasping sonship or living in the relationship with the Holy Spirit which Jesus describes in John 14. We are left in orphan-hearted Christianity where sadly the Holy Spirit (or more accurately our use of his gifts) accentuates that orphan-ness.

The Holy Spirit is not primarily given to enable us to "do", he is given to enable us to "be".

Again the danger we face is that our view of the Holy Spirit becomes like our incomplete view of Jesus; given to meet our needs and help us become better people. Once again it is only part of the story and the part which Christianity has grown up with over the past few centuries.

What we have therefore created is only a partial view of part of the Trinity, an incomplete concept of what is essentially a relationship. Our ideas have been good. Our understanding, in part, has been both correct and biblical, but nonetheless incomplete. Rather than seeing the Trinity as glorifying itself we have allowed our partial picture to focus on something more attuned to our own benefit or encouragement.

What then of the Father?

So far I have painted a picture of two members of the Trinity and my view of our incomplete understanding of them, their nature and their role in our lives.

God, the Father, seems to have been hidden. Why? Is he waiting for an appointed time when it is safe for him to reappear. Safe for who? Him or us?

I'm not a church history scholar but I wonder if, before the Reformation, the Godhead was seen as one entity known collectively as 'God' or the Almighty One very much like the 'Yahweh' of the Old Testament. The Reformation revealed, in part, the person of Jesus and the Pentecostal renewal revealed, in part, the person of the Holy Spirit. And so God, the Father, remains hidden and kept away from us
because we have believed the oldest lie that God is not good and nor can he be trusted. The lie which Satan sold to all humanity in the garden, "God is not for you, he is against you!" And so our Creator and the lover of our souls has been nowhere to be seen for centuries.

We have allowed our thinking to be limited so we only see Jesus and the Holy Spirit as persons on our side, sent to help us and to equip us. Sent to make us, one day, acceptable to the unknown member of the Trinity, the Father.

As Paul says we only see in part. That has been the limitation of the church and in many ways it will continue to be our limiting factor - "we see and understand in part". As the eyes of our heart are opened we begin to see things more clearly and the limitations we feel begin to be eroded as our understanding becomes more complete.

We are satisfied, or have allowed ourselves to be satisfied, with the partial truth and understanding we have created for ourselves. We have settled for something much less than the best that is on offer. We have tasted and allowed ourselves to be satisfied without eating the full meal and so our desire for more has been quenched. We have settled for the partial when the fullness is still to be grasped. In fact, Paul encourages us to enjoy all the fullness of God. That, to me, is a lot of fullness and a whole lot more than we have currently grasped. There is more, so very much more.

We have turned the Trinity upside down and inside out and have therefore only been able to find "roles" for two members. The members which we perceive as having something to offer us. Our needs being met and us being equipped to serve. The focus is on us and therefore on our servant hearted Christianity. "What can I do to serve God?" has been the cry of Christians and our church structures have sought to answer that cry through a variety of programmes and activities – many of which have been good and valuable but ultimately motivated by a lack of understanding as to the reality and completeness of the Godhead.

We find things for Jesus to do, we find things for the Holy Spirit to do. There are things that Jesus can give us, there are things that the Holy Spirit can give us. But what about the Father? What can he do for us? What can he give us?

The answer is blindingly obvious when we understand in our hearts **that God is love**. When our hearts fully grasp the magnitude of those three words everything changes. Because what the Father offers us is what we desperately need. It is the answer to the cry of every human heart.

What the Father offers is love. That is who he is and that word, love, represents the totality of his dealings with mankind.

We need love, specifically we need the Father's love. We need to know that we are loved as Jesus is loved, that God the Father is loving each and every one of us right now and that he is being a Father to us. Right now and every moment of every day.

This is what the mysterious third person of the Trinity has to offer, this is what he brings. **Love**. Perfect and complete unconditional love.

The reason, I think, that we have ignored him or left him out is because love is something we receive as a gift and we are not good at receiving. Orphans can't receive. We like to give. We want to be trained so we can serve and give (that's performance) but receiving is not something we do easily. In our orphan hearted Christianity it has been a foreign concept that anyone, particularly God, would want to give us anything. Why would he want to give us anything when our mindset since the time of the garden has been to work and strive in order to keep this untrustworthy master away from us.

So we do not embrace the Father because we feel we don't need, warrant or have earned what only he can give – Love. We need Jesus, we need the Holy Spirit but our orphan hearts tell us (lie to us) that we don't need to be loved. Yet, this is the very thing we crave, the very thing we were made for.

We have settled for this partial view of the Trinity because it feeds our needs. It feeds our longing to be useful and it makes us feel we are, in some way, appeasing the Godhead. What we have settled for is the belief that our ongoing salvation can only be the result or reward of our good works.

In some ways the church needs another reformation. We believe that it is by faith we are saved and our salvation is an act of grace. Once we are saved though, we have to work in order to maintain our salvation. Our view has become: *"it is not by works that we are saved but it is by works that we remain saved".* Orphan hearted thinking at its best!

We are closed to receive love as we don't see what value it can have to our driven lives.

It is only when we realise that, from its sad beginning in the garden, humanity is orphan-hearted that things can begin to change. We must not purely see humanity as orphan hearted but we must see the orphanness that is within our own hearts. It is the acceptance of our individual orphanness that starts the process of change. This recognition is the beginning of the eyes of our hearts being opened so we can begin to see things as they really are.

We have to face and see the orphanness in our own heart and in doing so we face and see the reality of our need of a Saviour. Not one who only saves us from our sin but one who also saves us from the emptiness of an orphan heart. We desperately need a Saviour who will fill the void in our hearts. A void that can only be filled with the perfect and complete love of our eternal and real Father.

When we face our orphanness we see our need for the third person of the Trinity. We see our need to receive love. We see our need to receive the only thing the Father can give us – his love.

As the eyes of our heart are opened to receive love then the orphanness within each one of us begins to reduce, decline and ultimately disappear. Gradually our eyes are opened to an amazing truth, an alternative way of living. We discover sonship. We start to see everything through a different set of eyes. Though, in reality not a new set of eyes, just all the wrong filters we have created being peeled away so we see things in the way they were meant to be seen. We see as the Father sees.

As sonship grows in our hearts we will inevitably turn our view, our partial view of the Trinity around into its more complete and true form.

We see a son who came from the Father not only to help us in our time of need but who shows us the way to the Father, not once but in an ongoing way. Jesus is constantly revealing the Father, he goes on doing it. The revelation of the Father by Jesus is not a one-off event which took place at the point of our salvation, it is an ongoing day to day revealing of the Father. Not only does Jesus constantly reveal the Father but he shows us how to live as a son or a daughter. In Jesus we have a living example of the spirit of sonship at work.

And so we begin to walk as Jesus walked not by copying everything he did but by having the same heart. A heart to please the Father in everything we do. A heart to please the Father that will break down the barrier between what we have called secular and spiritual. There is no distinction so far as the Father is concerned, he does not see two different personalities contained within one skin. He sees us as one person: a son or daughter. The distinction is man-made and it hinders our walk of sonship because we see one part of our life as being more valuable than another part. Part of us is therefore held captive and we do not see the spirit of sonship released fully into our everyday lives as we work in the office, work at home, or go about our daily business. This false distinction is man-made and comes out of a largely religious sense of duty and obligation.

We cannot create a spirit of sonship through our own effort. It is not a prize for living a good life. The heart of sonship is given to us when we receive the Holy Spirit of Sonship. It is his spirit in us that causes us to walk in his ways. It is his spirit in us which is the only thing that can ever enable us to walk as Jesus walked.

In fact "cause" may be too tame a word. I think the indwelling of the spirit of sonship is stronger than "causing us". I think it motivates, even drives us to walk as Jesus walked. We are not made to be clones, but as we receive the spirit of sonship we are enabled to walk like Jesus in a way which reflects our unique personality and character.

Receiving the Father's love is not a one off event but it becomes the central event of our daily living. Living loved. This is what the Father gives to us. This is the thing that we desperately need, this is the answer to the cry of the human heart. Yet this is the very thing we have stopped ourselves from receiving. In fact, we have been unable to receive it because the eyes of our heart have been closed to the state of our own heart.

Thankfully, the Father, by his grace and his longing for relationship, plants that seed of desire in our hearts which enables us to begin to see the orphanness of our heart. This desire sets in motion a longing for satisfaction, a satisfaction we find when we allow the Trinity to act as they love to act. To act in unity together bringing us into the full revelation of who we are.

So instead of seeing a Godhead which partially meets our needs we allow Jesus to turn away from us and back to the Father. We allow the Holy Spirit to expand his role from merely being a tool box to becoming the impartation and source of life within our hearts.

The Trinity therefore becomes a Father who we see through the eyes of the Son; a Son who reveals his Father to us and shows us that we are loved as he is loved. It becomes a Son who shows us our need of a loving Father and shows us what our lives can look like as we begin to walk as he walked. It becomes the Holy Spirit who pours the Father's love into our hearts which causes the spirit of sonship to grow within us. This Holy Spirit empowers us to walk in Father's ways because of the desire he plants in our heart. The Trinity is three individuals working as one in order that the life of Christ may be released in us so we would walk in sonship just as Jesus walked in sonship.

Instead of seeing only a partial Godhead we step into this vital life giving relationship. In a very real sense we become part of this mystical relationship as we are caught up and become "in Christ". Our gaze moves away from what we have to do or what we have to become and it turns to the Father who is the source of everything we need – **LOVE**.

This is the depth of love!

Chapter 10

The Substance of Love

When you want a cool refreshing drink of water you go to the tap, turn it on and fill up your glass. Or you go to the fridge, take out some fruit juice and pour it into your glass. You pour something into nothing and you have something.

That's exactly what it's like with Father's love. Romans 5:5 says: "God pours his love into our hearts through the Holy Spirit". God, the Father, pours the substance of his love into your heart. He pours something into nothing.

To fully understand this we need to remind ourselves of the nature and character of God. John writes and emphasises clearly in his first letter that **God is love**. Those three words sum up the nature and personality of God and tell us what he is really like. He is love. Everything about him is love, everything he does is from love and for love. His thoughts and actions for us all come from this heart of perfect and complete love. Everything about him is love, because **he is love**.

So when Paul writes that God pours his love into our hearts he is saying that the very nature and reality of who God is becomes a part of us. The substance of God's personality is poured into our hearts. God's own spirit becomes a part of our own spirit.

When you have an empty jug you pour nothing into nothing and you have ...... nothing. When you have a full jug you pour something into nothing and you end up with something.

As our hearts become open to the Father and to receiving his love the emptiness inside of us is filled up with the substance and reality of his love. He pours his love, his nature and personality, into our nothingness and we end up with something – the substance of his love.

We need to keep reminding ourselves of this truth: God is love. All of his dealings with us are simply because he loves us. His love for us is more tangible and real than any glass of water we may pour for ourselves. He is loving us with an everlasting love which will never run out.

Love is a relational thing. It is not a concept or theory that only works if certain rules are followed or obeyed. A relationship is flexible as it bends and yields to accommodate the other person. A relationship is two way and is based on giving and receiving, it will not survive if it is rigid or inflexible.

The Father is totally relational. We have already seen this in the beautiful and intimate relationships of the Trinity; relationships that we are invited to become a part of.

Our acceptance is not dependent on our actions or ability, it is not dependent on us following or obeying the rules. Our acceptance is simple; we are the beloved sons and daughters of the Father and therefore we belong.

We need to ensure that our experience of God is set in this context, the context of relationship where we know we are his beloved sons and daughters. We belong because we are his.

A relationship is living and organic. Religion is the opposite of relationship as it is stilted and static.

A living relationship creates a connection between two hearts and it is this connection which enables the substance of love to be transferred. I have a living heart connection with my wife and children which allows my feelings for them to be transferred from my heart to theirs. Our relationship becomes the channel for love to flow between us. It's the same with the Father. His relationship with us is the channel for the substance and reality of his love to be transferred from his heart to ours.

If our relationship with Father were governed by a set of rules then every time we did not achieve the required standard there would be a mark against us. A standard would be set that we could never reach and so our lives would be governed by performance and striving as we sought to reach the impossible target. This is the way many of us have lived for years!

A relationship is accepting and accommodating. Father accepts us as we are, Our failures do not disqualify us nor are they held against us. This is because our acceptance is not derived from our actions or behaviour but finds its source in the loving heart of our Father. We live in a relationship that is based on his unconditional love for us. In that safe and secure environment the very real substance of love is poured into our hearts freely and generously.

I often quote Romans 5:5 but it is a verse which used to annoy me until relatively recently. When you read it in its context it almost looks as if God's love being poured into our hearts is the logical result or reward of us enduring suffering, perseverance and character building. We go through sufferings, we persevere, we have our characters built and all we get is hope! We long for something more tangible than hope. This hope, we're told, is not supposed to disappoint us but I've noticed that a lot of people, myself included, constantly live with hope and are regularly disappointed because the things we've been hoping for do not happen. It seems that hope disappoints. Consequently we never get to the bit about God pouring his love into our hearts as we're stuck in the disappointment stage. This is what annoyed me: hope was not a reassuring thing but an ongoing disappointment.

But one day I turned it round and it became: "*Because God has poured the substance of his love into our hearts we are empowered to walk through sufferings, we are given the grace to persevere and consequently the fruit of the Spirit grows within us*". It does not end with love being our reward, **it starts with love**. It starts with the substance of Father's love being poured into our hearts. It starts with the foundation of a relationship which leads to us living the fruitful lives of sons and daughters.

Without a heart connection to the Father it is not possible for us to receive the love which he longs to pour into our hearts. It is not his ability to love us, for he is love, it's our ability to receive the love that constantly flows from his heart towards our heart. It's a heart connection which is not meant to remain static but one which goes deeper the more we are drawn into love. It's a heart connection which draws us closer into the heart of the Father and into the amazing relationship of the Trinity that we explored in the previous chapter. It is this heart connection that is the channel for the reality and substance of Father's love to be poured into our hearts.

When you pour something into nothing you get something. The love which Father pours into our hearts comes straight from his heart, it's not diluted or watered down on the way! We receive the concentrated, pure love of the Father.

The impartation of Father's love into our hearts was never meant to be a one-off event. It is something we should seek and desire on a daily or even hourly basis. We do not receive all the love we need when we are born again and so we need to go on receiving and allowing this love to change us. Love has an incredible power to transform and bring change as you'll have seen if you've watched the 'Sound of Music'. Maria starts working in the captain's house which has become devoid of love following the death of his first wife. Her loving personality and the joy in her heart is infectious and it's not too long before the children love her and the captain begins to let down his guard. He too receives her love and a family is transformed by the power of love. When love comes it can't help but transform. The law tries to change the external things of our lives and fails. But love is received in our heart and when our heart is transformed then everything changes.

Think about it. We take an antibiotic tablet when we have an infection. It's a real tablet. We take a sleeping pill when we want to sleep, it's a real pill. When we are hungry we eat food to sustain us and give us energy. It's real food. We drink a glass of water when we are thirsty. It's real water.

It's no different when we are talking about the Father's love. What we need and what we receive is the reality of the substance of

Father's love. It's the real thing – it is the transforming love of the Father being poured into your heart by the Holy Spirit.

As you read this you will all have had different experiences of the Father and his love for you. Maybe some of you are asking the question, "How do I receive this substance of love?" Others might be saying, "How do I go deeper?" In the next chapter I am going to look at how we go deeper and will tell some stories of friends of mine who have experienced this.

Let me explain how we can receive this impartation of love. Firstly, let me be very clear. The Father is loving you now, he has always loved you and he will always love you no matter what you might do or how you might behave. This has to be the foundation of our lives. His love is not dependent on us, it flows out of who he is. Our ability to receive may be limited but even that does not restrict the flow of his love into our hearts.

You know, there is a very simple prayer that Father loves to answer. We can pray it at any time of the day and it's best if we do it regularly. It goes like this: "Father, will you fill me with your love right now". He hears and he will answer. As we pray that prayer his love (the substance of who he is) is poured into our hearts and the more we receive the more change we will see in our lives. We feel loved, we experience love, we are being loved – this is the transforming power of the Father's love.

When we pray for people in our schools and conferences we pray that simple prayer because we believe it releases an impartation of Father's love into their hearts. It does not require a long prayer or ministry time. It simply needs faith for us to believe and to receive the truth that we are being loved right now by Almighty God who just happens to be our Father. God, the Father, is loving each one of us all of the time, the thing is we just don't know it. We don't experience it. If we have faith to believe then this simple prayer will release an impartation of Father's love into our hearts.

How much love can we receive? As much as we have faith for. This is why it is not a one-off event because as our faith grows we can keep coming and can receive a deeper experience of love.

The danger for us, is that by limiting our experience of Father's love we minimise it. If we think we have it then all we have done is brought it down to our human level of understanding. The Father's love is limitless and there is always more (so much more) for us to experience and live in. This is why we need to continually pray the prayer which he loves to answer "Father, fill me with more of your love".

The love of the Father is a real substance and if you are open to receive it you will not be disappointed. He pours this substance of love into our hearts. He pours the something of his love into the nothingness of our hearts in order that we can contain something and that something is love.

This is the depth of love.

Chapter 11

A Deeper Homecoming

A one-off encounter with the love of the Father is not enough. All of us need to experience an ongoing and deeper homecoming. As we have seen throughout this book the Father's love is not a static thing but it's the flow of living water that creates and sustains his life within us. If we choose to stay with our initial experience we will stagnate and, over time, the impact of his love will become diluted and before we know it we have settled back into our old way of life.

What we need is a deeper homecoming.

In 2002 I experienced the love of the Father which was a baptism of love that suddenly made a lot of things make sense. It was listening to a language I knew existed but one I'd never heard spoken. It was a homecoming. It was a realisation that I needed to step into Father's embrace and allow him to love me with his complete and perfect love. It was the beginning of a journey that continues to this day, one of living loved and knowing that God is being a Father to me.

I guess it was about six months after coming into this realisation of my need and subsequent revelation of the Father's love that I thought I knew everything there was to know about his love. It did not take too long to realise how wrong I was! There is so much more for us to discover and experience. In fact, if we ever think we've got it, all we have done is minimise the true extent of Father's love for us. The truth is we can never fully understand or appreciate the magnitude and depth of Father's love. It is simply unfathomable. All we can do is pursue it with all our hearts and seek to go deeper and deeper. As I said in the previous chapter receiving his love is not a static, one-off event but an ongoing life changing experience. It is something for us to explore and continue to receive with all our heart.

As we conclude this journey of discovery my encouragement is to pursue this with all your heart. James Jordan likens it to a bookshelf. We collect various 'books' of Christian experience such as worship, prayer, ministry, teaching, children's work etc. These are all books that need to sit on a bookshelf. The foundation of the

Father's love is that bookshelf. It's the same in our families; we collect various 'books': children, finances, holidays, the garden, work etc but these too need to be on a bookshelf. The bookshelf of Father's love. What I have seen over the years is that many people start out by making the Father's love the bookshelf of their life but after a couple of years it has slipped into being simply another 'book' that now sits on the shelf of busyness, activity and performance.

It is only as we pursue the Father with all our heart that this revelation and impartation of love becomes and remains the bookshelf of our life.

Keeping this revelation and relationship central means we need to keep bringing our heart home. We need to keep experiencing a homecoming. We need to experience a deeper homecoming which takes us further into the extravagant love of our Heavenly Father. We need to keep drinking from the life-giving water which Jesus promised. We need to maintain a living and organic relationship rather than letting what we have experienced become settled and static within us.

Recently I have read Mark Stibbe's new book "Home at Last" in which he describes the trauma he went through as an eight year old boy when he was 'abandoned' at boarding school. For his first year Mark had a brutal and sadistic housemaster and so various events and circumstances caused him to close his heart. He calls this a 'boarded heart'. As he describes his experiences at boarding school he highlights a number of bereavements such as: being deprived of love, home, safety, childhood, siblings, innocence and freedom.

I, too, went to a boarding school though, for me it was only for six years from the age of twelve. Whilst the majority of my memories from that time are positive I could identify with the various bereavements Mark lists and which he explores in some detail. Despite knowing and trusting that my mother was doing the right thing I missed her and my sisters, my home and the wider church family we were surrounded by. My school house had a strict timetable (regulated by the house bell), it had rules that were unyielding and despite being run by a godly couple it lacked the sense of family that I was so used to. I soon discovered the only way to survive was to play the game by the rules. This I did and became good at. My heart, like Mark's, became a boarded heart and I know I chose to close my heart as I believed it was the only way to protect it.

I know I had a homecoming in 2002 as I brought many of those experiences and feelings to Father. I know I began to experience him loving me and for the last fourteen years this journey of love has deepened and grown within me. Yet as I read Mark's book I realised I needed a deeper homecoming as it was now time to bring some of those bereavements to Father.

Our journeys are all unique and our experiences all different. But I have come to see that if we are to live in love we need to keep looking at the state of our heart to see which areas remain closed. Our Father is jealous for all of our heart as he longs to pour his love into every part of it. He can only do so if our hearts are open or become open to the impartation of perfect love. If the bookshelf is to remain the bookshelf we need a deeper homecoming. We receive love and we go on receiving love. We receive comfort and we go on receiving comfort. And so do not be afraid when things come up in your life, take them to Father and let that part of your heart come home. Allow **your** boarded heart to experience its homecoming.

This is the depth of his love for you.

I first met Sarah a few years ago in Uganda. That was the start of her journey into Father's heart where she could feel safe enough to open up all the pain which had been locked away for many years. As this journey began Father gave her a promise that her heart would be filled with colour, a promise which has come true over the last three years. Let Sarah tell her story:

As I let go, I fell into his arms and felt the safest I have ever felt. This was the starting point of my journey into the depth of love, a journey that I'm still on. Father was taking my ripped heart and restoring it using fine, beautiful, coloured threads.

Since that first encounter, when a yellow glow filled the room, the Person of Love has revealed colours to me as I've allowed him deeper into my heart. Soon after yellow came green which was an encounter of being found. The redemption of a little girl, and indeed an adult, who always hid herself, and yet he stooped down into every hiding place to whisper "you were never lost to me but always found".

As I came to him with that childlike response and opened my heart, not only was he able to take me deeper into the pain but he also took me deeper into a revelation of who he is and who I am. I can only describe it as pure love. For the first time, instead of tears of pain, came tears in response to perfect love.

On each encounter with love he has given me a new colour. I now have nine colours which sounds crazy but I feel them in my heart.

More recently, his love has taken me to deep comfort. Whilst at Inheriting the Nations School he showed me desperate areas of my heart that were void of comfort. The emptiness I felt, together with years of self-harm, had left me feeling such shame and yet he came to me with his mothering love. At first, because the emptiness seemed fathomless, I had no sense of his presence but somehow my heart knew he was filling the void. This encounter came in the midst of my deepest fear. As Father held me in his gaze fear went and I experienced comfort. Deep, soothing, rich comfort.

In a way, my homecoming has been a series of homecomings as my heart has been restored and filled with colour and life. I know that his desire is for my whole heart and, as I continue to experience a deeper homecoming, I will discover more of this vast, amazing love. Living in the Father's love is sonship. Being completely rooted and grounded in his love is the source of everything and from here will come the overflow of life.

Amazing! This is the depth of love which Sarah has experienced and you, too, can experience that same love. As it has for Sarah, living in love can change everything for you as well.

As Nelson Mandela said "It's a long walk to freedom" and very often that's what it's like for us. Although we think our journey begins when we had an encounter with the Person of Love it actually began before we were conceived in our mother's womb. God has always been our Father and he planned and knew each one of us before the beginning of time. He does not make mistakes.

Listen to Michael's story:

My long walk to freedom started about forty years ago in South Africa, the land of my birth, and continues to this day as I open my heart to more of my Father's unconditional love. I remember having a divine encounter with Love when I was six years old as I ran straight into the arms of my Saviour, Jesus. I knew I was His as I'd met the One who calls me by my name.

I grew up in a Christian home where I knew my parents loved God and had a desire to live for him and serve him. I, too, had this sense in my heart but I quickly learnt that love was not unconditional. I thought that in order to please God I had to earn His love. Religion taught me that God was always angry with me and that I could never live up to his standards. Love was earned and not freely given. This foundational structure in my heart, coupled with many years of sexual abuse as a child, caused me to close my heart to the love of my parents and the love of my Heavenly Father.

After many years of confusion, struggling with same sex attraction, living in a homosexual lifestyle and searching for love in all the wrong places I knew the only answer to my brokenness was back in the arms of the One who created me. I had another very powerful encounter with Love as I found a community of believers and made this wonderful church my home. I quickly slotted into the life of the church but my significance was still determined by what

I did for God and not in who I was. I am very good at doing and so I began to do even more. Little did I know that I was heading for a major burnout.

Tired and exhausted, I did an A school in London. This was the beginning of the undoing of me. I wept for a week. The deep revelation of sonship turned my world upside down and inside out. I saw something that I had never seen or heard before. I was awakened to the reality that if God was my Father, then I was His son. I knew this with my head, but now it became alive and real in my heart. Knowing that I was my Daddy's child propelled me onto a journey of coming back home to him. To the place where I'd always belonged, deep within His heart. I felt like I was born again, again.

Everything fell apart as my foundations were shaken and the things I held dear were turned upside down. I ended up in New Zealand on the Inheriting the Nations School where this revelation of sonship began to take root in my heart. I began to know deep in my heart that I was unconditionally loved. Loved not for what I could do but loved for who I am. I was loved in my weakness and in my brokenness. I no longer had to seek healing, which I had pursued all my life, but now I could just be a son and receive the love of my Father and everything would flow from that. I could lie down and receive and that was enough. No more, no less. A life of being, not a life of doing. I could breathe. I could be free to be me. I had come home.

The undoing continues. The journey has been filled with highs and lows. Now my life looks nothing like I ever dreamt it could be. A deep peace and contentment has settled in my heart. All my foundations of what I once knew have been shaken and are falling off me and a new reality is emerging. Whatever the future holds, I know that I am His beloved son in whom he is well pleased. I AM HOME.

As God is our real Father I believe there is a longing in our hearts to come home. We will not find that home through our activity or busyness but in the unconditional love of the Father where we hear him say those words: "You are my beloved son", "You are my beloved daughter". As Michael says, we find it in our 'undoing' when all the fig leaves are stripped away and we are able to step into unconditional love. This is a journey and one which can last the whole of our lives simply because the love of the Father is unfathomable.

Helena, together with her husband Eric, has been on this journey for many years. Over the years as Father has taken Helena deeper into the ocean of his love she has found that there are always new depths of love to explore.

It's now been eighteen years since my first revelation of God as my Father. It was not as if the lights suddenly came on and everything was different, for me it has been more gradual. Little by little as I listened to Jack Winter and James and Denise Jordan my heart began to open as I walked in forgiveness and let Father work on my heart.

Sometime later we took on the leadership of the church which was a season of hard work as we had a young family and the church was going through some changes. This ended with me suffering a burnout and wondering whether God even existed, let alone him being a Father to me. I could no longer believe nor trust as the ground beneath my feet had been swept away. I didn't know if I would ever return to that place of knowing him as my Father. I doubted myself: did I ever receive this revelation? Was it real? Have I imagined it? I just didn't know. During this season I consciously stepped back from leadership and Fatherheart Ministries.

Slowly rest came. Little by little the desire to be vulnerable came back. Over and over again I would hear the doubts saying I wasn't good enough but the desire was so strong that I went searching, seeking a deepening relationship with him, looking for life to flow once again. And so I went to a B school in Finland and drank from a stream of living water all week. The hunger in my heart grew even more.

The next stage of my journey was to spend a month in New Zealand. A whole month to wrestle with Father and all the questions I had. A month to deal with the doubts.

*At the end of the month all I could say was YES. There **was** a foundation in my heart, it might have been buried beneath the dust but it was there. I'd taken a long trip around the world but my heart finally came back home. It's a home that's so familiar it's like resting on your favourite couch, a place to belong and to rest. During that month I went from revelation to revelation, the penny dropped and my heart went to a much deeper level. Now I know that I really know!*

My desire for more revelation has grown since that month away. Knowing that the revelation of

Father goes so much deeper than this makes me very happy. It doesn't stop with the revelation of today as I will continue to know Father on a much more intimate level and that won't stop until the day I die. That makes me hungry for more!

This is the depth of love. An ongoing, deepening relationship with our Father. As I've already said if we ever think we understand his love all we have done is minimise it and brought it down to the capacity of our mind. His love is fathomless and there is no end to the depth of his love for us. Let us keep seeking, desiring and exploring this love.

I hope you are beginning to see that our experience of love is an ongoing one where we continue to live and go deeper in this amazing love. It's a journey that will never wear us out or exhaust us. It's an exciting one as we discover more of the nature and personality of our Heavenly Father. It is journey that has no limits as his love for us is immeasurable. We can never fully fathom its depth. In 1998 Barry Adams had a life changing encounter with this Father, one that led him to write the Father's Love Letter and one that threw him unexpectantly onto a global stage. Let him tell his story:

In 1998 a simple hug from a man named Jack Winter transformed a broken hearted and performance driven thirty seven year old man into a much loved son.

Even though I had been a Christian for twenty two years and had been serving in full time pastoral ministry, I didn't really understand the true meaning of why Jesus died for me. Until that moment, I had assumed that my new birth into the Kingdom of God was about me becoming a more effective servant in the hope that, one day, my service would make me acceptable to God.

But when Jack put his arms around me and prayed that his arms would become the arms of my Heavenly Father, I had an encounter with Love that changed everything. At that moment I knew I was a son and this was irrespective of anything I did.

This new revelation of love catapulted me unexpectedly onto a global stage after my sermon illustration called 'Father's Love Letter' went viral on the Internet. Before too long, I was being invited to travel internationally as well as managing the increasing demands of my vision to see this love letter delivered around the world.

I wish I could say that my relationship with Abba remained unchanged through the explosive growth of my 'ministry'. After all, when I discovered that Almighty God was my real Dad, I realized that this was the answer to my lifelong heart's cry to be a son to somebody. But unfortunately that was not the case. Instead of simply learning to live the life of a much loved son, my devotional life was being scrutinized by the masses on the Internet and by people who would hear me speak at churches, conferences and schools.

It wasn't long before I started to carry the weight of the world on my shoulders again. I felt responsible to meet the demands and expectations which were being placed on me and so the joy I'd felt of being a little boy with a big Dad gave way to other things. I didn't know it at the time, but I needed a deeper homecoming or should I say, multiple homecomings.

The truth is, over the past 18 years, I have had

many encounters with the love of my Abba that have re-centered me on what is really important. This is that I am a much loved son to my Dad. These encounters with his love usually come in the times when I feel I least deserve it.

In the past 2 years alone, I have experienced multiple encounters with my Abba's kindness that have brought comfort and courage in the midst of some pretty daunting circumstances after our youngest daughter was diagnosed with Leukemia in September 2014.

I know him as the Father of Compassion and the God of all comfort in a way now that I have never known Him before. He has been with me and my family every moment of every day as we continue the long road to our daughter's complete recovery.

I fully expect that as I continue this journey, there will be many more encounters that will simply point my heart towards home in order that I can keep the main thing, the main thing!

And that is, I am a much loved, little boy with a really big Dad.

Keeping the main thing, the main thing! How

easy it is for us to let that slip and instead of living in the amazing love of our Heavenly Father we slide back into our old ways of performance and striving. Instead of being rooted and grounded in love we allow fear to take over and, once again, we begin to believe the lie that our acceptance to God is based on our activity for him. We lose sight of the main thing.

Through the redemptive work of Jesus we are no longer orphans. We are the beloved sons and daughters of our Heavenly Father. He is, and always has been, our Father. We are loved with the same love and passion that he has for his son, Jesus. We belong.

This is the depth of his love for us.

"I have revealed to them who you are and I will continue to make you even more real to them, so that they may experience the same endless love that you have for me, for your love will now live in them, even as I live in them"
(John 17:26 TPT)

Afterword

I am very grateful to Julie Graham, who has done a thorough job in editing this book and correcting my many mistakes of grammar and punctuation. Thank you Barry Adams for writing the foreword and your encouragement to share about the depth of love the Father has for each one of us.

I am especially grateful to those who have contributed their stories and in doing so have expressed a vulnerability of their own hearts. Sarah, Michael, Helena and Barry – thank you. (If you would like to listen to Sarah's story in full go to: http://www.afathertoyou.com/webcast-video/2016/2/11/sarah-davis-testimony-10th-february-2016.html)

Here are details of other resources you may want to look at as you live in the Father's love.

A Father to YOU - www.afathertoyou.com
Audio and video teachings, teaching materials, inspirational videos and details of events in the UK.

The Father's Love Letter - www.fathersloveletter.com
An intimate message from God to you, in over 80 languages.

Fatherheart TV – www.fatherheart.tv
Inspirational videos and live webcasts to inspire and help you grow in the love of the Father.

Fatherheart Ministries – www.fatherheart.net
The ministry of James and Denise Jordan with details of the International schools and other events. Complete with online store with excellent teaching resources.

If you would like to go deeper on this journey of love then I recommend books by James and Denise Jordan, Trevor Galpin, Barry Adams and Stephen Hill.